Also published by Arktos Media:

Can Life Prevail?
A Revolutionary Approach to the Environmental Crisis
by Pentti Linkola

Metaphysics of War:
Battle, Victory & Death in the World of Tradition
by Julius Evola

The Path of Cinnabar:
An Intellectual Autobiography
by Julius Evola

Tradition & Revolution:
Collected Writings of Troy Southgate (2nd ed.)

A

HANDBOOK

OF

TRADITIONAL

LIVING

TRADITIO

ARKTOS MEDIA
MMX

Published in Italian as *Il mondo della Tradizione* and *Unità operanti per il Fronte della Tradizione*. Originally published in 1997 and 1998, respectively, by Ass. Cult. Raido.

First Edition English edition 2010 published by Arktos Media Ltd.
Translation Copyright © 2010 by Arktos Media Ltd.

ISBN **978-1-907166-06-8**

BIC classification: Philosophy of religion (HRAB); Revolutionary groups & movements (JPWQ)

Translated by S. K.
Edited by John B. Morgan
Book layout and typesetting by John B. Morgan
Cover design and artwork by Andreas Nilsson

ARKTOS MEDIA LTD

www.Arktos.com

CONTENTS

PART ONE:
THE WORLD OF TRADITION

PART TWO:
THE FRONT OF TRADITION

TRANSLATOR'S FOREWORD

S.K.

The publication of the present booklet serves two complementary purposes: a) to present the reader with an accessible introduction to the world of Tradition; b) to offer ideal guidelines to those already active in the arena of revolutionary politics. Parts One and Two of this volume were originally published separately in Italy, under the titles of *Il Mondo della Tradizione* and *Il Fronte della Tradizione*.

Part One sets out to define Tradition as that eternal source of spiritual and normative values which infuses the lives of individuals and societies with meaning and dignity. Its authors touch upon the chief aspects of the traditional outlook: the notions of metaphysics, esotericism and initiation, caste and authority, cyclical decline and renewal. Traditionalist values are here set forth as a bulwark against the onslaught of profoundly disruptive forces:

> The rejection of all injustices, lies and illusions gives rise to two fronts: if falsehood is the tool of Subversion, truth is the victorious weapon of Tradition. Truth is not a human product, but exists independently of individuals, whose duty it is to grasp it and realise it by means of action in the world.

That of action is the path advocated in this volume. The reader, therefore, should take note that the exposition of traditional doctrines it presents is closely tied to the personal equation of the authors, who have followed the legionary example in choosing as their motto *Vita est militia super terram:* 'Life is a soldier's service upon this earth.'

Given its *kshatriya* inclination, Raido is not a writers' guild but a *base militante:* a local community formed of individuals seeking to uphold the values of Tradition through active social and political engagement. When this writing was first published some ten years ago, it was primarily to educate the young political militants in the ranks of the Italian radical Right.[1]

The approach to Tradition presented in this booklet, therefore, is unabashedly Evolian. There is nothing in these pages that Julius Evola would not have subscribed to and perhaps a few things that traditionalists of a different disposition might take issue with. This is particularly the case with the meta-historical narrative presented in § 7 of Part One, which is almost entirely based on *Revolt Against the Modern World.*

Far from being a drawback, the Evolian twist of this work offers the reader who is new to the world of Tradition a concise introduction to the meta-historical vision of one of its great Twentieth century spokesmen. The Evolian direction of the first half of the volume also sets the pace for Part Two, where an attempt is made to relate the values of Tradition to the active fight against Subversion in contemporary society.

The reflections articulated in Part Two have their roots in decades of challenging political activism: in a desire to learn from past mistakes and make a clean break with sterile ideologies. The suggestions and models proposed by Raido, and inspired by the legionary example of the Rumanian Iron Guard, are applicable to all traditionally orientated communities. Yet, if the education of the political soldier remains

---

[1]   For more information on Raido, which continues to publish books, distribute traditionalist material and organise conferences in Rome, visit the website www.raido.it.

the most explicit aim of this work (originally issued as part of a series on "The Formation of the Militant of Tradition"), its teaching is far more broadly applicable: for the unfashionable notions it invokes – of Loyalty, Love, Justice and Truth – are as relevant to the life of the lone wolf as they are to that of the man of militia. The Front of Tradition, regardless of what external form it might take, is first and foremost an inner condition: a greater jihad to be waged at every moment against the enemies within.

A NOTE FROM THE EDITOR

JOHN B. MORGAN

All footnotes to the text, unless otherwise attributed, appeared in the original Italian editions. In some instances where quotations from other texts are used, I have used the relevant passages from existing translations. These are always cited in the accompanying footnotes. Wherever quotations are used I have attempted to provide a bibliographical citation – if a citation is lacking, this means that I was unable to identify its source.

FROM THE PREFACE
TO THE SECOND ITALIAN EDITION

We have received much encouragement in publishing this small yet essential piece of writing, which seeks not to be exhaustive, but rather to offer militants a chance for reflection.

The aim of this writing is to awaken an enthusiasm for Tradition among those of a similar disposition and to foster the kind of personal development capable of distancing militants from all forms of modern perversion. It is our firm belief that without a clear point of reference it is difficult to escape the vortex of decadence, which, in the long run, might end up devouring even those who are in principle opposed to the crisis of the modern world.

It is often the case that one's actions lack a clear direction; that a person lives his life from day to day, either enmeshed in the quicksand of barren intellectualism or a sacrificial victim to pointless agitation. The militant is thus either trapped in an ivory tower or ready to tackle any social issue in an attempt to prove himself up-to-date: in both cases, he remains unaware of the reality that surrounds him.

In *Revolt Against the Modern World,* Julius Evola argues that 'to leave the parameters of Tradition meant to leave the true life. To abandon the rites, alter or violate the laws or mix the castes corresponded to a regression from a structured universe (cosmos) back into chaos'.[2]

Tradition acts as a norm: as an internal and external law to be followed, particularly in moments of crisis such as the present one. As a measure and norm,

---

[2]   From *Revolt Against the Modern World* (Rochester: Inner Traditions, 1995), p. 55. (Ed.)

Tradition must first of all shape our lifestyle and help us distinguish between friends and foes.

For this reason, traditional doctrine cannot be imposed: it can only be chosen freely in a conscious act of inner development. While a person may prove unworthy of his aspirations or fall before an obstacle, what matters is to be able to rise again and face difficulties with renewed determination.

Tradition is for the militant the necessary support to meet the challenges of everyday life. The militant must be clearheaded and conscious: respect for truth and justice, and Nature and its laws, will be the tangible signs of his connection to that transcendent Order which envelops the man in his entirety.

INTRODUCTION

The present text is conceived as a means of awakening the values of Tradition in the hearts of the young. It is not simply another product for the enjoyment of intellectuals incapable of translating the ideas they prattle about into action. The pages that follow contain a summary of the crucial elements of traditional doctrine; far from being exhaustive, they aim to provide a starting point for further individual development.

Today more than ever before the moral crisis is visible in every aspect of life. In the realm of politics, culture and even religion, the profound malaise that affects individuals – and, by extension, society as a whole – is all too evident. Politicians, philosophers, fanatical fans of progress, trendy ecologists and fake gurus are all competing to come up with new catchwords in the attempt to remedy a situation that has become desperate. Far from providing any remedy, however, their actions contribute to foster those subversive tendencies that plunge man into an even greater crisis. Such people are like those doctors who prescribe the wrong drugs through mistaken diagnoses.

The person we are addressing, by contrast, is of a very different sort: his 'style' is based on the values of loyalty, fidelity, honour and sacrifice.

Loyalty serves to establish correct relationships between individuals. While modern man, trying to be clever, resorts to meanness and falsehood, the man of Tradition acts in accordance with the principle of truth. A valuable example is given by C.Z. Codreanu,[3] who

---

[3] Corneliu Codreanu (1899-1938) was originally a lawyer who began agitating against democracy and Communism in the new Rumanian state after the First World War. In 1927, he founded the Iron Guard, or the Legion of the Archangel Michael, a militant revolutionary group deeply imbued with Rumanian Orthodox mysticism. After he became a threat to the existing regime, he was arrested and executed. Evola, who met him

states: 'Leave the path of infamy to others. Better to fall in an honourable fight than win by infamy.'[4]

Honour and fidelity serve to measure one's inner disposition. The two values are closely related. To act with honour is to follow the norms of one's community: the genuine meaning of the term should not be confused with its modern usage, which reduces it to a merely exterior form of behaviour. Fidelity, through references to an absolute and universal Order, elevates honour to a higher dimension.

Sacrifice is the virile aptitude to offer oneself. Every action that invokes the principles of loyalty, honour and fidelity is elevated to the status of ritual: it thus becomes a sacred action, which presupposes the overcoming of those instinctual bonds which condition human nature.

Conscious of the fact that present reality stands in opposition to the traditional way of life, we are also aware of the many attacks seeking to disrupt the journey undertaken by the individual who aspires to differentiate himself from the masses. It has become increasingly difficult to defend the positions gained on the path of honour, and the risk of losing the fruits of years of sacrifice is great.

> What genuinely and exclusively matters today is the work of those who know how to stand on the summit: those who are resolute in adhering to their principles, unalterable, indifferent to the frenzied convulsions, superstitions and betrayals of the latest generations. What matters is only the steadfastness of the few whose unmovable,

---

once, was most enamored of him and his movement. (Ed.)

[4]   Corneliu Codreanu, *For My Legionaries* (Reedy: Liberty Bell Publications, 2003), p. 244. (Ed.)

iron presence can establish new relations, distances, and values: while they will not prevent this world of deviants and madmen from being what it is, they will nevertheless pass on the feeling of Truth to others. And this feeling, perhaps, will one day trigger a liberating crisis.[5]

Like an iron presence that gives in not an inch to this world, we must prove steadfast in the face of the illusions and refined cajolery of the enemy. What differentiates us from the enemy is our style: the possession of a genuine character and inner discipline. This is what shapes our reconstructive radicalism, which in Tradition finds its source of energy and legitimisation, in action its path.

---

[5]   Julius Evola, *Revolt Against the Modern World*, pp. xxix-xxx. (Ed.)

PART ONE:

THE WORLD OF TRADITION

1
FROM THE ORIGINS
TO THE MODERN WORLD

In common parlance, the term 'tradition' is now used to denote customs or habits. When the word is invoked, it is to refer to what belongs to a remote past, the memory of which only survives in folklore. One example of this is Christmas: only the consumerist aspect of the feast is found today, so that for most people it has lost the sacred meaning it originally possessed. By no means, however, is this the meaning of 'Tradition', a term which embodies eternal, holy and incorruptible values.

The first thing to be emphasised concerning the world of Tradition is that it is founded upon a union or effective link between divine reality and the human, and between spirit and matter. This unity is not affected by the divergence – unique to the modern world – between sacred and profane.[1] According to Tradition, participation in the realm of the holy represents the foundation of all life, personal as well as collective, expressed through a constant drive towards what lies above. Nature itself, with its rhythms and laws, is here envisaged as the visible manifestation of a higher rhythm and order. No real separation exists between Heaven and Earth, God and man: only a degree of 'similarity', whereby the former is reflected in the latter. According to traditional doctrine, the phenomena and forces of Nature are to be perceived as the expression of a higher reality, as symbols that

---

[1] This fundamental truth finds confirmation in everyday life: just as a body nourished with healthy food shows signs of health and well-being, so the person who performs his duties in line with the values of Tradition will reap the orderly fruits of his actions.

can explain non-human knowledge. Given this premise, it can be argued that traditional man, unlike modern man, possesses a symbolic and spiritual rather than elementary perception of Nature. Understanding of the symbols of Nature provides a support for those who wish to embark on the journey upwards.

Rather than being based on the materialist and progressive utopia of 'evolution', traditional civilisation expresses an opposite truth: a vision of cyclical eternity. From noble beginnings, through the passage of time, involution takes place. A fall from original perfection occurred through the degradation of man who was not – as modern evolutionism would have us believe – a brutish creature, but rather a better being than what he is now: a 'supra-man' or demigod. While modern science, based as it is on the subversive theory of evolution, holds that humanity progressively evolved from lower to higher levels, according to traditional culture humans fell from their originally superior condition to an increasingly earthly and material one. Such a fall, brought about by the prevailing of human, mortal elements, is recorded among many peoples as the 'dimming of the Gods': the retreat of heavenly influences and the growing incapacity of many to draw these powers to themselves.

Two ways exist, then, in which to envisage and interpret History: on the one hand, there is the modern and progressive perspective, which sees time as the ordering of successive events that can be quantitatively measured and arranged according to a numeric and chronological sequence; on the other, the traditionalist perspective, which is cyclical, symbolic, and which emphasises the rise and fall of civilisations. The Ancients' view of History as divided into four eras can be discerned from Hesiod's[2] *Works and Days*. As Hesiod illustrates, time, for the Ancients, did not pass uniformly and indefinitely, but was rather divided into cycles and periods, each of which possessed its own meaning and specificity. Every cycle differed in terms of duration, and the sum of all cycles formed the totality of time. The various periods were symbolically represented by different metals – Gold, Silver, Bronze and Iron – according to the relation of each era with the beginning of the cycle. The four metals listed symbolically embodied a process of spiritual degeneration spanning four cycles or generations. As already mentioned, according to this perspective, humanity originally existed in a state similar to that of the Gods and later degenerated into forms of social life dominated by impiety, greed, violence and deceit. Perfect in the beginning, humanity later experienced the separation of warrior and priestly power, which was then followed by the rule of the merchant class (bourgeoisie). In such a way, the unity of the primordial Principle was broken and a process of involution occurred.

The above truth is attested in many Holy Scriptures, which preserve the memory of human origins as something resplendent and immortal. These Scriptures speak of a mythical race existing in eternal light, forever in contact with cosmic and divine forces. At that time pain and toil were unknown, the earth generously yielded abundant fruits, and humanity was free from death and old age. Men in this age were wise and happy: they 'knew and could'. The primordial age, known as the 'cycle of the Watchers', had its centre in the far North, the 'evergreen, luminous Land of the Watchers'. This was the homeland of the Hyperboreans, variously

---

[2]   Hesiod (approx. 7th century BC) was an early Greek poet. (Ed.)

5

known as Thule, Avalon, the White Continent, the Garden of Eden and the Golden Age, from whose roots all civilisations have sprung. In this era one could speak of 'men similar to Gods and Gods similar to immortal men'. Men and Gods, in the primordial era, lived in complete harmony, as truth and justice ruled supreme.

The original race of the Hyperboreans called itself the Arya, the noble ones, who possessed an Olympian and regal nature. Some of the symbols associated with this era further contribute to reveal its values: the Axis, Steppingstone, Centre, unreachable Heights, Life, Fire and the Sun. At a given time, the unity between divinity and humanity was broken, and man fell increasingly under the spell of material forces. Devoid of any higher point of reference, man began facing the insecurity and angst of everyday existence. His initial loyalty and uniformity were progressively lost, leading to the dawn of the modern world.

The historical memory of ancient peoples suggests that transition from one era to another was characterised by genuine cataclysms. One undeniable example is provided by the inclination of the world axis and the climatic changes it brought about. The memory of this event is preserved in many traditions, which tell of a mythical ice age that made the Hyperborean homeland inhospitable, forcing its inhabitants to leave. Symbolically, the inclination of the world axis represents the fall, spiritual alteration and loss of the 'Centre' (i.e., the loss of origins).[3] As a consequence of this fall, what had previously manifested itself was obscured; the first age, the Golden Age or ancient Cycle yielded to the second: the Age of Silver or Atlantic Cycle. This was still a noble era, albeit an undoubtedly less regal one than the first. It is in this age that religion

---

[3]   By using an analogy, the inclination of the world axis can be said to correspond to that of the heart axis in man.

emerged, in its theistic, devotional and mystical forms, as a reaction to the loss of the primordial condition (the term 'religion' derives from Latin *re-ligo,* to reconnect or tie again). Symbols associated with this era are the moon, night and the serpent (standing for fecundity), which embody the female principle. Woman, as mother, is chosen in this age as a generative symbol, while the male aspect of divinity is conceived as mortal. Society at this time is regulated by the priestly principle, while the regal function is confined to the political sphere: thus commenced the separation of political power from spiritual authority.

The cycle, however, does not end here: the Silver Age yielded to the Bronze, also known as the Titans' Cycle. This phase is characterised by the affirmation of wild and materially inclined virility, the spiritual element now having been secularised.[4] Genuine authority no longer exists in this age – the age of violence and usurpation – only power affirmed by means of force. Finally comes the Age of Iron or 'Dark Cycle', that of our time, in which injustice, death and pain rule supreme. This age is ruled by economic power: man is entirely devoted to the pursuit of 'prosperity at all cost', to the point of forgetting his relation to the divine. Dark forces expressing the unleashing of materiality now take over. The regal function, naturally occurring in the Golden Age, has now withdrawn and is no longer visible. A fifth age should be added to the four just mentioned: the Age of Heroes or Aryan Cycle, which will lead to the restoration of the Golden Age. This final cycle signals the overcoming of the preceding phases and the establishment of a new link with the sacred

---

[4]   Institutionally, 'secularisation' represents the measure taken to turn a cleric into a layman. The expression 'process of secularisation' is currently employed to describe the progressive fading of the religious element in the life of individuals and societies.

origin. The duty of the man of Tradition is to act in order to secure that this era may see the ranks of the Front of Tradition ready to face its dark enemies and achieve final victory.

2

TRADITION AND THE SACRED

Divinity is normally envisaged by contemporary man as an abstract and distant entity that is no longer present or active in everyday life. Ours is a world stripped of sacredness, where everything is sacrificed on the altar of production and mass consumption.

The term 'sacred' is used to denote not only that which transcends man, time and life, but also that which eternally exists. The sacred, therefore, is 'that which links earthly life to invisible supra-natural forces': an order governed by laws higher than man, which is oriented towards the divine.

Etymologically, 'Tradition' derives from the Latin *tradere,* a verb formed from *trans* (= 'beyond') + *dare* (= 'to hand over'); hence, it indicates the act of passing something over and should be understood as 'that which is transmitted'. Tradition consists not in the conservation or consolidation of exterior appearances or of things the meaning of which is no longer understood: Tradition rather indicates the direct and effective transmission of a heritage that is non-human and essentially spiritual in origin. Traditional action means dynamic action: its transmission presupposes a link between giver and receiver, the latter being responsible for the perpetuation of the ancestral heritage. Across generations, this heritage takes the form of an ordering power that pervades the whole of reality, transcending the merely material and biological side of existence.

It would be correct in this context to speak of an 'Immanent Transcendence': of a spiritual force, that is, which operates as a living, dynamic and creative presence through institutions, cultures, customs, laws, religions and the like, making spiritual and supra-individual values the axis and supreme point of reference for the general ordering of things. This allows underlying principles to be passed on from one age to another, in such a way that all human actions may uniformly be directed upwards, in line with a general ideal.

To identify oneself today as a man of Tradition is to be committed to the transmission of the received heritage for the benefit of future generations.

3

METAPHYSICS

The term 'metaphysics' (deriving from Greek *meta* = 'beyond' + *physis* = 'nature') is used to describe that which is situated beyond what is visible and merely human: that which transcends what falls under the influence of the senses and is conditioned by the limits of time, space and transient nature.

Time and space identify materiality, which is limited by those conditions that constitute its nature. For beyond the world of sensation it would be incorrect to speak of time, space or any other limitations. According to traditional doctrine, matter and becoming correspond to that which changes and can be identified with disorder, multiplicity and division, i.e., the world

9

that is subject to the cycle of birth, growth and death. By contrast, that which is sacred is associated with being, order and harmony. The sacred, in the mind of those capable of feeling and recognising it, constitutes the most genuine expression of reality: a model handed down by divinity, ancestors or mythical heroes, which must be accepted and scrupulously followed. When the sacred is lacking, what remains is something transient, illusory and meaningless.

Tradition is eternal, universal, and open to all those capable of understanding and experiencing it. Diversities in language, customs, laws or religions do not contradict the underlying unity of Tradition. What changes is only the way in which Truth is expressed: as its essence remains unvaried, each traditional form can be seen as a specific adaptation of the primordial Tradition out of which all traditions derive. This adaptation has occurred in order to make Truth accessible to peoples that inhabit different places and possess different characters.

Tradition has no beginning and no end: it always was and always will be, and will maintain its validity and legitimacy in all ages and lands. What is eternal should not be confused with that which is perennial and lasts for a long time: what is eternal is situated above time and cannot undergo any possible change.

4
THE STATES OF BEING:
ARCHETYPE-SOUL-SPIRIT-BODY

According to Tradition, all Beings find their origin in a primordial and unitary Principle. This Principle has variously been described as Archetype, Supreme Being, Divine Will, Prime Mover, etc. The Supreme Principle is universal and undetermined: it represents absolute unity beyond all qualification and distinction, the common source of matter and spirit that transcends both.

The metaphysical Principle is both One and All: it is the One that is All and the All that is One. The Principle resolves all oppositions; as the origin that precedes all things, it removes multiplicity by uniting and merging all dichotomies (good/evil, love/hate, light/darkness, beginning/end, etc.).

The metaphysical Principle cannot be understood in rational terms, for reason is conditioned by time and hence unsuitable for the comprehension of what is eternal. Despite their efforts, modern scientists are lost when facing the harmony and order of the cosmos. The Principle 'is "without duality", and outside of which there is nothing, either manifested or unmanifested.'[5] It is actually impossible to describe the Principle, for it possesses neither name nor form: by its own nature it cannot be expressed, for any definition would limit it. It would be better to say of the Principle, as the root

---

[5]   Réné Guénon, *Man and His Becoming According to the Vedanta* (Hillsdale: Sophia Perennis, 2001), p. 72. It is worth noting that in its original context, Guénon is equating this Principle with the Vedic concept of Brahman. (Ed.)

11

of all things, that 'it is not this' than to provide a false and partial representation of it.

The Principle is situated on an invisible, absolute level, yet operates in the world as a divine model and divine will. This second universal level is that of the soul, the supra-natural entity situated above all individual beings, whether material or psychical. While transcending individual forms, the soul also belongs to individual creatures, which it allows to partake in the divine, which is to say: in universal Being, the principle of all existence. The other two modes of existence instead belong to the level of individuality: one is the spirit, the other the body.

The spirit – or psyche – represents the subtle compound of immaterial vital forces; it includes memories, impulses, feelings, perceptions, pleasure, pain, fear, love, hate, habits, desires, instincts, etc. The physical body is the gross material substance, the external sheath of being possessed by terrestrial and material forms of existence.

For the man of Tradition, the individual embodies a transitory and contingent manifestation of genuine being. Human life, therefore, is merely one among an indefinite multitude of states belonging to the same being, which is entirely independent of all its manifestations.

The combination of body and soul gives rise to the ego (individuality or the contingent I), which represents a horizontal projection of man. The spirit, by contrast, constitutes the personality, the higher I or self of man: his metaphysical and eternal core, his vertical dimension and genuine being. According to this tripartite division of human reality (soul-spirit-body), the man who is ignorant is ruled by passions: having forgotten his true nature, he is identified with the ego, which chains him to his psycho-physical dimension.

The man of Tradition thus feels the need for inner development. In order to achieve such a goal, the individual must strenuously work on the level of his own body and spirit in order to sever the ties that bind mortal humanity. A process of ascesis is required to break free of all materiality by developing clarity of mind and adopting a discipline that is the visible manifestation of an acquired style and inner order. A thorough job is needed to remove all defects, such as egoism and self-interest, and replace them with positive traits. By operating on one's body and spirit it is possible for each individual to attain a subtler dimension of living: the dimension of the soul.

5
ESOTERICISM & EXOTERICISM

All traditional systems articulate their doctrines on two levels: one a popular, external level (exotericism); the other an inner, symbolic and allegorical level (esotericism). The latter expresses the highest and most essential character of any doctrine: it concerns metaphysical teaching and is revealed to a minority alone, a necessarily qualified elite capable of understanding it. The elite preserves a body of metaphysical and transformative doctrines that allow the individual to effectively attain spiritual knowledge.

No contrast exists between esotericism and exotericism: far from being opposed to one another, the two levels are different expressions of the same doctrine. In the symbolism of the Cross (see Appendix I), exotericism is represented by the horizontal axis, esotericism by the vertical one: the two levels and opposite directions contribute to form a single truth. That of exotericism is the level of religion, religious dogmas, devotion and emotion, which never leads beyond individuality and includes that which is elementary and can be accessed by most men. Hence, every religion is adapted to the conditions suited for given peoples in given ages. While a degree of religious intolerance can occur in the realm of exotericism, no such thing can occur on the level of esotericism, for esoteric doctrine is one, universal and eternal.

While exotericism often supports religious fundamentalism, esotericism always affirms the transcendental unity of religions and traditional forms. The symbolism of the mountain can be seen to convey this reality: 'Many paths lead upward, towards the same goal'.[6] Such a view, which emphasises unity, should not be confused with 'syncretism',[7] or – worse still – with the kind of forgery of the sacred that is promoted by neo-spiritualist movements like Theosophy, Anthroposophy, ufology and occultism. At best, syncretism and neo-spiritualism lead to the superimposition of elements of different origin, which are merely brought together by human agency. These pseudo-religious paths exploit and mangle the rules and symbols of different traditional forms, leading their followers to ruin.

To remove oneself both from the company of religious fundamentalists, who foster fratricidal strife, and 'd.i.y.' neo-spiritualists is one of the best steps that any man mindful of traditional specificities can take in order to

---

[6]   The various traditional forms are but many paths allowing man to reach the ultimate goal of the sacred. (This is a well-known Chinese proverb. It is also sometimes told as 'Many paths lead to the top of the mountain, but the view is the same.' –Ed.)

[7]   The term 'syncretism' is currently used to describe any action seeking to reconcile diverse and antithetical philosophical or religious positions.

avoid falling victim to subversion. For it is precisely these two phenomena that subversion encourages: the clash between followers of legitimate religions and the spread of neo-spiritualist beliefs.

6
AUTHORITY

Tradition is synonymous with truth and justice, as it represents the affirmation of order against the falsehood and rebellion that inform a modern view of life.

Another characteristic of Tradition is its direct link with authority, a term deriving from the Indo-European root *aug-* = to increase. Tradition brings to mind the notion of authority, which is directly connected to Imperium: sovereign, ordering force. Imperium is that power bestowed by divinity, which is connected to virtue and kingship – the figure of the king embodying political, military, legislative and religious power. One example of Imperium is aristocratic society, in which authority creates a natural distinction among men according to the value, role, vocation and quality of each person.

Authority engenders hierarchy, from the Greek *hieros* = 'holy' + *archè* = 'principle', 'order': the order which situates the best men above all others. Each man is a small universe unto himself; as such, he is identical to none but himself. Hierarchy and selection measure and regulate this diversity: 'For in some superior men is effectively to be found what in others exists merely as a confused aspiration, foreboding or tendency, in such a way that the latter are inevitably attracted to the former, and take on a subordinate role.'[8] It is the inferior, after all, that stands in need of the superior.

Hierarchy is not a bureaucratic scale ascending according to seniority; rather, it follows traditional principles. At the summit stands he who better than any other embodies these principles, knowing how to assimilate and apply them: he is the *primus inter pares,* the first among equals, he who possesses greater qualities. On the one hand, therefore, we find a minority formed by a quality elite; on the other, quantity. The greater the quality, the fewer the people who possess such values. The basic principle of authority is its sacred nature, which derives directly from God. Authority, which embodies order, peace and harmony, is expressed through a hierarchy in which each person, aware of his own position, can actively take part in the organic life of the State.

This organic vision allows separate entities (individuals, families) to contribute harmoniously towards the whole (the community or State), in such a way that each man may preserve that degree of autonomy necessary to develop his own specificity and nature. By rejecting any abuse of one part against the others, all fractures and forms of atomisation are avoided. Each man is thus free to develop his own self according to his nature and in line with his vocation, this orderly vision strengthening rather than limiting the potential of each person.

---

[8]   Julius Evola, *Hierarchy and Democracy* ([Gerarchia e Democra-zia], Ed. di Ar, 1978). (No English translation exists.-Ed.)

7
CASTES

The ideal, organic and traditional State is regulated by four castes: priests, warriors, producers and servants. These castes symbolically correspond to the division of the human body into head/brain (priests), breast/heart (warriors), stomach/liver (producers) and limbs (servants).

Traditional order is not fanciful, and division into castes is not simply an arbitrary product of human will. **It is not one's birth that determines one's nature, but one's nature that determines one's birth** – and, by extension, one's caste. Caste means law and order, for it is considered the starting point for any attempt at spiritual elevation. Every individual has a share in the universal Order and supra-natural Principle by remaining faithful to his own nature and caste. In a social system directed upwards, the nature of each being is hierarchically ordered according to justice, so that every inequality among men is made to reflect a deeper inequality: each person, having found his place, observes the ancient law that states 'to each his own'. Every human activity, on the other hand, offers the same possibility of spiritual elevation: to fulfil one's duty is to contribute to the implementation of Order and hence to partake in the metaphysical Principle.

The political and social reflection of this perspective can be found in the organisation of the Indo-European peoples, who divided their own communities according to three chief functions corresponding to the three aspects of being (soul, spirit and body) – the fourth function being reserved for servants. The first function corresponds to the mysterious administration of the universe, with its divine laws and rituals, and embodies the affirmation of a general cosmic order in the world of men. This is the function of priests, who guard the primordial and holy knowledge and actualise the sacred by means of ritual. Priests, repositories of those techniques used for consecration and sacrifice, stand as the mediators between sky and earth, the sacred and humanity.

The second function embodies power and command, virility, heroism and that force which grants victory; through action, it brings about the regeneration of the universe. This is the warrior caste expressed by the aristocracy: that power and energy which acts in defence of the community.

The third function, which symbolises fecundity and prosperity, is shared by the majority of the people: producers, farmers and artisans. These people are responsible for the activities connected to the securing of those goods and services needed by the community.

Above all castes stands the King, the embodiment of the unity of spiritual authority (priests) and political power (warriors). The King is the heart of the world, the living reflection of its origins, the intermediary between sky and earth, and a creature possessing both a human and a divine nature. The King stands at the summit of the human hierarchy, as the last step in the celestial hierarchy and the worldly, visible manifestation of a higher order: as the Lord of peace and justice. The King expresses all three functions: he is the sovereign administering the law, the warrior who protects the community from enemies visible and invisible, and the giver of peace and prosperity. The order which the King embodies can be broken if he fails in his duty: pride, deceit and lust are the chief causes that bring decadence about by upsetting harmony and balance.

When decadence first took its course, kings were replaced by priests. As spiritual authority became separate from temporal, a lunar form of spirituality came to prevail, and the virile element assumed a passive role before the female (embodied by Demeter).[9] This decadence allowed priests to be invested with power that was neither regal nor sacred, but merely material and secular. In such a way, the twin phenomena of religious abstraction and the secularisation of power first occurred. This was the age of warriors, who in a titanic revolt sought to affirm the principle of war through the sheer use of violence.[10] In the Classical world this savage element is symbolised both by the amazons,[11] who embody the devious attempt at lunar restoration, and by the figure of the 'superman', who represents a materialistic virility that acts under the influence of pride, violence, perversion, passions and instincts. In place of Authority we find here a power that affirms itself by means of violence. With the

[9] Demeter was one of the most important deities in the Greek world. The goddess, who embodies the generative power of the earth, was originally worshipped in agrarian cults. Later the figure of Demeter acquired a deeper significance as the expression of death and rebirth in the natural world. Along with Demeter, the cult of feminine deities and the religious sentiment of devotion survived. In Rome, the goddess took the name of Ceres.

[10] 'Titan' is the name given in Greek mythology to each of the six giant sons of Uranus and Gaia who sought to conquer Mount Olympus but were defeated by Zeus. The term is used to describe any form of rebellion against divine order (which imposes both laws and limits). The hero who fights and dies for the affirmation of the divine order thus opposes the titanic attitude that ignores hierarchy and hampers the path to the heavens.

[11] According to Greek mythology, the amazons were warrior women who lived in a community from which men were excluded. It is said that amazons used to amputate their right breast in order to draw their bows more easily (the term 'amazon' is formed by *a* = 'without' + *mazon* = 'breast'). The amazon symbolises the usurping woman who loses her spiritual femininity by going against her own nature and making a parody of manly virtues

advent of the merchant caste, instead, a utilitarian view of economy came to permeate all aspects of life: wealth and material gain thus became the highest ideals. In Classical thought this change was embodied by the passionate lover Aphrodite[12] – who replaced the figure of the Mother – and by Dionysus,[13] a symbol of licentiousness, orgiastic outburst, excess and the primacy of sex and death.

The prevailing of the servant caste, with its darkness, has led to the folly of collectivism, of anonymous masses and pure shapeless quantity, which embodies the loss of any contact with Heaven. A possibility exists, nevertheless, to halt this fall by restoring the origins by means of the warrior element. Heroes can newly conquer the primordial condition and give birth to a new 'Golden Cycle' by achieving immortality. Spiritual virility can only be attained by overcoming both material virility – the Titans – and lunar spirituality – Demeter. Heroic civilisations represent the restoration of the original light. The Titan stands for the raw fabric of the hero: both figures partake of the warrior condition, but while the drive towards transcendence is aborted in the case of the Titan, it is fulfilled in the hero. According to Tradition, there is no conflict between spiritual authority and temporal power; rather, the

---

[12]   According to Greek mythology, Aphrodite is the goddess of love and beauty. Aphrodite was worshipped under various guises reminiscent of the Semitic goddess Astarte-Ashtar. While symbolising sexual, profane love, Aphrodite had originally been perceived as a powerful and terrifying deity, associated with natural instinct and the power of procreation in all their violence. Aphrodite thus embodies the female principle of generation, which outside hierarchic order represents a destructive and subversive force. In later centuries, Aphrodite was set in contrast with Urania, the goddess of intellectual, heavenly love.

[13]   Dionysus was the Greek god of wine: the Dionysiac state is characterised by inebriation and excitement. F.W. Nietzsche identified this as the dark and passionate side of the Greek spirit, opposed to the Apollonian.

two are bound in an organic and hierarchic relation. When the two functions are instead set in contrast with one another or separated, a cycle of decadence begins: a cycle destined to end with the complete rejection of all authority.

8
CIVILISATION

Civilisation is born of the union of man with the divine and represents the balance between political and spiritual values, the former being hierarchically ordered and made subordinate to the latter. Modern culture, by contrast, has developed from purely human, earthly, egoistic and utilitarian elements; replacing hierarchy and difference with levelling uniformity, it inevitably perceives decadence as the motor of history. Traditional civilisations, while different in appearance, share the same underlying values, for they are founded on spiritual forces and ideals that embody the highest point of reference for the organisation of society. In traditional civilisations primeval power imparts order to lower forces, which are thus moulded and united. When this power loses some of its original strength, the lower forces break free and take the upper hand, engendering destructive phenomena that set decadence in motion.

Civilisation is the highest expression of all communal spiritual forces operating through political organisations and the processing of those elements inherited from Tradition. For this reason, in all traditional civilisations the governing of the state is in the hands of the best man or men: with each individual striving for perfection, a hierarchical pyramid or scale of values is formed.

In the world of Tradition, political and social forces are in direct contact with invisible ones, to the point that they constitute genuine religious orders. In such a way, social order is made a tangible manifestation of a higher order in which a classification of rights and duties is drawn on the basis of individual qualities and responsibilities. Now that similar relations between human communities and the sacred no longer exist, chaos prevails. However, any elite that embodies genuine values and actualises them in everyday life gives rise to a new aristocracy (a term formed from the Greek *aristos* = 'the best' or 'most fitted' and *archè* = 'beginning', 'order', 'command'). This aristocracy, capable of distinguishing friends from foes, embodies values on the basis of which it can examine both others and itself; as such, it provides a new way of experiencing life. Traditional values exist independently of the beings through which they were made manifest and endure unchanged as a repository of ethical examples capable of giving rise to new forces and identities. The best way to pass on this way of living is by embodying the values of the spirit in everyday life, as living examples for others. The rejection of all injustices, lies and illusions gives rise to two fronts: if falsehood is the tool of subversion, truth is the victorious weapon of Tradition. Truth is not a human product, but exists independently from individuals, who nevertheless have the duty to grasp it and realise it by means of action in the world.

9
HOLY WAR:
VITA EST MILITIA SUPER TERRAM

It is important to understand that being (that which is) stands in contrast to becoming (that which changes), just like light to darkness, knowledge to ignorance, life to death, justice to abuse and violence, love to hate and spite, order to disorder, and the virtue of honour and loyalty to cowardice and disloyalty. These oppositions represent the qualitative expressions of two fronts perennially in battle to conquer the world: Tradition and subversion. 'According to this doctrine there is a physical order of things and a metaphysical one; there is a mortal nature and an immortal one; there is the superior realm of "being" and the inferior realm of "becoming". Generally speaking, there is a visible and tangible dimension and, prior to and beyond it, an invisible and intangible dimension that is the support, the source, and true life of the former.'[14]

Men engage in this battle by siding with either one of the two fronts. On the one side stands the noble and honest man: the saint, hero, and artisan, who is a master of himself and seeks spiritual affirmation; on the other side stands the sly, cowardly, wretched loser incapable of inner self-affirmation. Tradition helps man discover his true conscience and dignity; it allows man to awaken his metaphysical essence and to accomplish his transcendental mission through actions in everyday life. Man must feel an utter loathing for falsehood: he must prove loyal and above all petty self-interest, in such a way as to preserve a higher dignity, a love for

---

[14]   Julius Evola, *Revolt Against the Modern World,* p. 3. (Ed.)

what is essential, coupled with an ability to consecrate any action performed. Only thus can man newly erect those bridges to the sacred that the folly of modern egoism has destroyed.

It is necessary therefore to seek a new affirmation of the spirit and to wage what Tradition describes as the Greater Holy War: the inner fight against the enemy who resides within each man. This is a profound, immaterial struggle that each person must undertake against greed, rage, fear, cowardliness and instinct. Life thus becomes an eternal fight between spiritual forces and their opposite: between solar forces and the dark forces of chaos and matter. The Greater Holy War is waged between the Solar Principle in man, the self, against what is merely human, weak and subject to passions: the I or ego. The Lesser Holy War, instead, is waged against external enemies: barbarians, those who do not belong to one's community. The Lesser Holy War is cathartic,[15] which is to say: it favours the emergence of an inner enemy. The two paths should become one: he who in the Lesser War experiences the Greater will overcome the 'death crisis' by ridding himself of the inner enemy and of the instinct towards self-preservation. Once fear, desire and restlessness have been overcome, man becomes free of all instincts and afflictions. An Eastern text explains that: 'Life is like a bow, the soul like an arrow, the Absolute like a target: one must reach the Absolute like an arrow reaches its target.'[16] In such a way, the path of the warrior and the

---

[15]   The term 'catharsis' derives from the Greek *katharsis,* meaning 'purification'.

[16]   *Markandeya Purana* 42.7-8. (Evola references this same passage in *Revolt Against the Modern World*, p. 123. A more literal translation of the original reads: 'Life is [Brahma's] bow, the soul is his arrow, Brahma is the target sublime. It is to be pierced by the heedful man; he should be united with Brahma, as the arrow *becomes embedded in the target.'* From *The Markandeya Purana,* translated by F. Eden Pargiter [Calcutta: The

ascetic meet: war, no longer a mere show of force and destructive violence, becomes an action performed with love and detachment, a discipline and style founded upon the values of truth, justice, fairness, honour and loyalty.

Vita est militia super terram, 'life is a soldier's service upon this earth': this will be the motto of those who turn to Tradition as their guide and affirm the primacy of law, order and hierarchy; of those who choose the sky over the earth, day over night, opposing the family and state to mongrel promiscuity, and blood and race to equality.

Tradition thus also stands for the preservation of the memory and identity of one's folk,[17] which must constantly be renewed. Subversion, by contrast, represents oblivion: the loss of identity, and the rejection of any continuity with the past and any future prospect. The man of Tradition must always seek to defend this sacred order, striving with all his might to oppose chaos and injustice.

Asiatic Society, 1904].-Ed.)

[17]   The word 'folk' is commonly used to describe the inhabitants of any geographical or political area sharing the same language, customs and beliefs. The traditional understanding of this word, however, is quite different. The notion of 'folk', like that of 'nation', only becomes significant and partakes in a higher order of existence when it is integrated within a hierarchic, organic state. Only in the context of a traditional state does the folk – a physical and spiritual extension of the family – become something more than a mere biological entity. It is worth quoting here the words of Julius Evola: 'Our ideal must be seen as our true fatherland. What matters is not whether we share the same country or language, but whether we share the same ideal. This is the essential starting point. To the collectivist unity of the nation . . . we oppose an order of men who are loyal to the principles of a higher authority and legitimacy, principles that stem from our ideal.' This is how we envisage the folk: as a folk made of men of Tradition.

10
DECADENCE & SUBVERSION

In the *Tao-té-ching,* Lao Tzu writes: 'When the Way
has been lost, there comes virtue; when virtue has
been lost, there comes morality; when morality has
been lost, there comes justice; when justice has been
lost, there comes social custom; custom, a mere shadow
of plain form (ethics), is the beginning of disorder.'[18]
Decadence is a degenerative process that coincides
with the moment in history[19] when spiritual values are
replaced by ideologies, which are founded exclusively
on a socio-economic mechanism. On the one hand we
find legitimate power, spiritual authority and a divine
force directed upwards (which is to say, an anagogic
force: from the Greek *anagogia,* literally the act of
weighing the anchor, of elevating oneself); on the
other, a force directed downwards: a cause responsible

18   *Tao-té-ching,* text 38. (Ed.)

19   In world history, there are times when the process of decadence
manifested itself in particularly explicit ways, times that marked the trau-
matic passage from one epoch to another. From a wider perspective, the
previously described doctrine of the four eras tells of the passage from
the Golden Age to the present Iron Age, when the loss of spiritual values
led to the progressive spread of materialism (something all too evident
nowadays). Within this cycle, it is further possible to isolate some historical changes of momentous significance for the European world: the fall of
the Roman Empire, the fall of the Holy Roman Empire, the subversive
values of humanism and the Renaissance, the Enlightenment and Positiv-
ism, which ultimately led to the greatest catastrophe ever to have befallen
mankind: the French Revolution. Following this event, to which the decadence of the French nobility contributed, subversive phenomena occurred
at an ever-increasing speed through the spread of democracy, capitalism,
Communism, and the actions of powerful occult manipulators. Following
this chain of events, we reach the present day, in which Satanic elements
like abortion, genetic engineering, and the blossoming of new spiritualist
cults are perceived as ordinary phenomena.

for the degeneration and eclipse of civilisation. Disorder within civilisation occurs, therefore, when a disintegrating power prevails that is founded upon matter and chaos rather than Order. Two verbs can be seen to express this opposition: 'to be' and 'to have'.

Hindus call the Golden Age *satya-yuga,* the age of being that corresponds to the primordial origin and is opposed to the age of illusion. The latter is the age of possession ('having'), for it is marked by the prevalence of economic and material problems. According to this perspective, besides the world of nature and ordinary perception two other levels of reality exist: one the supra-natural, directed upwards; and the other is the sub-natural, which leads downwards, to the nether regions.

The process of subversion has followed various stages, all of which are linked to one another. The first step in the process was to turn Tradition into mere conformity and social custom: a collection of historically inherited norms and institutions of no real value. The next step for the agents of subversion was to deny the validity of all spiritual influences, thus blocking the upward drive in man. This was made possible thanks to the spread of various cultural and political theories that employ materialism and atheism as their initial tactic. Rationalism, egalitarianism, evolutionism, utilitarianism, relativism, individualism and economism are nothing but single components of the same subversive plan, the aim of which is to nullify any human aspiration towards the sacred. Once all links with Heaven had been severed, and a veritable barrier had been erected against divine intervention, a process of **solidification** took place.[20] The only

[20]   'Solidification' is the term used by R. Guénon to describe the process of the materialisation of being. Guénon specifies that this process occurs when man, no longer in contact with the divine, replaces the sacred outlook on existence with the material, which is subject to

27

direction followed then was downwards, towards
regions governed by irrationality and infernal forces.
This phase, which is characterised by the dissolution of
personality, is even more dangerous than the preceding
one: for now those individuals who feel the need to
'react' in some way are offered **surrogate forms of
spirituality,** which invoke traditional ideals while
distorting their genuine meaning, to the point of
betraying their original message. Modern man, who
lacks the guidelines provided by holy law, falls under
the spell of neo-spiritualist movements and sects
without realising that these counterfeit and subvert
genuine spirituality. This pursuit of irrationality
frustrates any attempt to react against the crisis of
the modern world, thus neutralising any reaction at
the hands of those who still feel the need to cultivate
their own 'inner dimension'.

The true aim of subversion is to overthrow legitimate
spiritual sources by confronting them with an increasing
number of obstacles, like materialism, in such a way
as to overthrow divinity. It would be absurd, therefore,
to seek to improve social life while overlooking the
integral formation of human personality (body, spirit
and soul). All genuine political reforms or revolutions
are in fact spiritual reforms and revolutions.

11

INITIATION

The word 'initiation' derives from the Latin *initium* =
'beginning' and *in ire* = 'to enter', and is connected to
Janus, the Roman god of beginnings. In turn, 'Janus'

demonic forces.

is etymologically connected to *janua* = 'entrance door', the embodiment of beginning, the starting point of the process of self-realisation that leads to the transcendence of the human condition. The initiate is the *Pontifex:* he who erects a bridge linking Heaven and Earth, and embodies the synthesis of regal and priestly power. The *Pontifex* is seen as he who is capable of conducting rites that 'support' the community and foster contact with the divine world. The initiate is a royal figure, the intermediary between God and man, who stands at the summit of the human hierarchy and at the basis of the heavenly one. The initiate is 'born of Heaven', for as the point of conjunction between the divine and human worlds he is a bringer of light.

In order to understand the concept of initiation it is first important to grasp that Being includes various levels of existence both above and below the human one. Thus, human personality can either ascend towards the highest Being or fall until it reaches the sub-human and animal level. Ascension constitutes a veritable *rebirth* leading to the transcendence of the human condition and its limits. This process transforms the whole individual in order to establish a contact with higher levels of being. Rebirth represents a radical change, a move from one state of existence to another: the acquisition of a new kind of awareness through the passage from darkness to light brought about by the transmission of a spiritual influence that leads to freedom from all necessity. In order for this process to prove efficacious, an 'external' intervention is required: the transmission of a spiritual influence conveyed by ritual means within a regular, legitimate initiatic organisation. Such an organisation must be linked, whether directly or through other centres, to a single supreme centre; this centre, in turn, must be part of the unbroken chain of the Primordial Tradition. The individual seeking to pursue the path of initiation must naturally be inclined in that direction (or else, any effort on his part would be in vain).

Three essential qualities are required in order to walk the path of initiation: the first is qualification, i.e., power (the power to act); the second is transmission, i.e., virtue (the ability to make one's power active and effective); the third is the capacity to untiringly perform constant work on oneself, i.e., actuality (constant awareness of one's actions).

Initiation, therefore, has nothing to do with an egalitarian or democratic outlook, with morals or religion. Its aim is not to make man free of sin, but to visibly bring about a transcendent power. Religion emphasises the distance between creatures and their Creator, and envisages the former as dependent upon the latter and devoted to Him. Initiation instead does away with these limits: it replaces the notions of salvation and redemption with the concept of **awakening.** Besides the world of those who *believe,* there is the world of those who *are.* Metaphysically there is no such thing as good or evil: only that which is true and real and that which is false and illusory. What is real is what the soul experiences when it is united with itself: the individual then finds himself 'living' in a condition of certainty and fullness where he requires nothing and feels no need for agitation and speculation – an eternal being in possession of itself. Higher reality is free of the need to satisfy wishes, instincts and feelings; it knows no bounds, whether external or internal. When this reality is rejected, the individual is dragged down when his inner power goes to sleep. The meaning of any genuine ascesis is the conquest of that which has been lost: a vivification of the primordial condition which neutralises the negative influences exercised by the instinctual and irrational part of the human being, while strengthening his Olympian nature. The *awakened one,* the initiate, knows no thirst, fever, temptation or anxiety: free from all desires, he has gained a different kind of awareness. The initiate inwardly belongs to a different world, one that is no longer agitated or subject to necessity and the rule of the senses. The initiate becomes immortal. This path too, however, is strewn with dangers. Besides an initiation that opens the gates of Heaven there is counter-initiation, which drags man into the abyss of Hell. Counter-initiation represents the deviation of all aspirations towards pure spirituality: a current that clouds the vision of Truth, falsifying all values and fostering infernal influences.

12
CONTEMPLATION & ACTION

Tradition teaches that there are two paths leading to initiation: contemplation and action. Both paths represent opposite poles of the same spiritual reality open to those who wish to embark upon the journey towards self-realisation.

Contemplation embodies the realisation of Truth: an impulse towards the One, the supreme archetype, that is attained by distancing oneself from the reality of the senses. This direct perception of the highest reality is attained through death and the transcendence of what is merely human. Such knowledge extends beyond all human means – beyond reason and feelings – and can be obtained through separation and ritual purity by freeing oneself from the bond of individuality. Contemplation means participation in the divine reality that transcends all limits and mundane influences, and ultimately embodies the foundation of the priestly caste.

The second path to initiation is action. This path operates within the world: he who embraces it does not shun the sensory realm of activities and struggles, but at the same time is not attached to the goals and fruits of action; rather, this person will assign the same value to victory and defeat, pleasure and pain, by placing his own actions above love and hate. A life thus experienced will *transcend life:* it will awaken an inner tension in the individual that, by overcoming the lower self, will lead to a state of light and power capable of vanquishing all that is merely human and physical. Such a condition allows the individual to partake in sacred reality by embracing heroic, warrior values.

The Primordial Tradition itself is above and beyond the division of these two paths, which are ways of approaching ultimate unity. The two paths of contemplation and action derive from regal and priestly initiation: they respectively embody the warrior, heroic Tradition and the priestly Tradition. In order to embark on either of these two paths the complete integration of all human faculties is necessary. Contemplation is to action what the sacred is to the human, the eternal to the transitory, spiritual authority to temporal power. Traditional doctrine, however, does not envisage the two paths as being in opposition to one another; rather, the two paths are seen as distinct and separate in their functions, like kingship and priesthood.

13
LAW

Tradition cannot be historicized through references to past events, nor can it be seen as merely a human invention to be freely manipulated. Tradition is neither an ideology nor a philosophy; nor is it a way of thinking or a human whim. Tradition is not a remembrance, but rather an expression of creative will and power. By conforming to the laws of Tradition, human nature allows Tradition to manifest itself again and again as a living reality. It is man's duty to adapt his own behaviour and way of life to traditional principles. In such a way, Tradition becomes a dynamic drive to create and conquer: a tension leading to higher goals which causes reality to conform to the divine will.

Those who are not in a position to ignite the sacred fire can envisage Tradition as a support, as law and loyalty. Tradition thus acquires its normative character, as a sacred law that allows all individuals to partake in supreme reality in accordance with their own nature. The basic principle followed by the Indo-European peoples was of a divine order sustaining the whole universe. Law was seen as something bestowed by the Gods upon humanity in order for man to avoid all impiety and injustice through adherence to traditional values. The primary function of juridical institutions is to affirm divine order in human society in such a way as to favour a connection with the 'power from above'. In traditional societies conscious obedience to law is perceived as a support that allows the individual to conform himself to a universal order where no separation exists between the human and religious dimension. All life in traditional societies follows divine rhythms and laws. In such a context, there is no difference between a religious decree and a juridical precept, as all legitimacy is derived from an imperative power both eternal and spiritual. To transgress law in traditional societies is to oppose that which is sacred.

He who follows Tradition remains faithful to his *ancestral heritage* by perceiving the divine in all moments of his life, thus bearing witness to the values of truth, justice, loyalty and honour. Inner dedication to traditional principles leads to a genuine awareness that shapes one's life by infusing it with a higher significance.

14
RITE

Humanity possesses the means to enter into contact with the Primordial Tradition and to regenerate the sacred action that lies at the basis of life.

Rite, myth and symbolism represent three means of touching man's heart in order to awaken his inner powers. These three realities embody veritable bridges or 'umbilical cords' linking Heaven and Earth: three means to implement sacred order. In such a way material elements like blood and soil undergo the influence of the spiritual element, which vivifies and renews their original power. Traditional knowledge thus operates through rites, myths and symbolism.

The term 'rite' is etymologically connected to the Sanskrit *rtá* = 'order'. It represents the action which re-establishes contact with the divine world of the origins and allows individuals or the community to partake in the sacred order. Rite thus links man to the *archè* (the Greek term for the principle of life): it annuls the progression of time by again evoking the original act. In such a way, in any era rite is rendered actual and operative. Rite essentially means sacred action – the term 'sacred' being connected to the Latin *sacer facere* ('to make sacred') – and embodies the reaffirmation of the mystery of life as the spiritual heritage of man. The aim of rites is to put human beings directly in contact with a divine reality that transcends individuality and unites the members of a community. Rite represents the application of the supreme law which re-establishes order and halts chaos. It stands for loyalty and is a means of partaking in the supra-world which makes reality a visible mirror of the divine order. Rite represents man's experience of divine reality: it is a moment of joy and love in which the original force uniting man to the sacred is reinstated. Thus, by symbolically overcoming death and renewing life, rite becomes the very creative principle of life. In traditional communities, where all is governed by sacred norms, private and collective relations are mediated by laws closely connected to ritual action. The efficacy of ritual is only guaranteed when it is performed in conformity with those rules that secure its validity, by scrupulously respecting conditions both objective and subjective.

If a rite is altered, it no longer has the power to actualise the primordial energy, and thus turns into ceremony: a merely human action devoid of any contact with higher reality.

15
MYTH

The term 'myth' derives from the Greek *mythos* = 'announcement', which is a cognate of the Latin *mutus* = 'mute' and *musso* = 'to keep silent', 'to conceal' (suggesting the difficulty of understanding myth).

Myth embodies absolute truth, as it expresses a sacred event that occurred in the primordial era. Founding myths represent the point of reference *par excellence,* which engenders institutions and norms that cement political communities.

Myth is what allows individuals integrated into the cosmos to live an orderly life by regulating their everyday actions (from eating to marriage, work, art, agriculture, hunting, sexuality, etc.). By emulating in his everyday activities the archetypal exemplar of myth, man abolishes profane existence in favour of a magical-religious life centred on an eternal present. In the chaotic changes of history, with all its contradictions, myth stands as an eternal dimension, as a model that accompanies and guides man by providing firm points of reference. Myth is a sacred (as opposed to profane) narrative that illustrates truth allegorically, explaining all that which cannot ordinarily be explained as it lies beyond mere reason (for instance, the origin of life, the destiny of man and civilisation, and the causes of its ruin).

Myth is the narrative of a meta-historical order, a narrative that tells of the hidden powers which influence visible human reality and reveals how inexplicable events came into being. Myth integrates history with meta-history: it is through myths that the actions and lives of individuals receive a suitable orientation. Once their true value and meaning are lost, myths become mere mythological tales, fables, and expressions of folklore which remain in the popular imagination.

16
SYMBOLISM

The term 'symbol' derives from the Greek verb *synballo* = 'to unite', the opposite of which is *diaballo* = 'to divide', from which stems the word 'devil'.

Symbols are the visible expression of a supra-sensible reality: an immediate way of conveying Truth. Sacred knowledge is expressed through symbolism, through images capable of awakening the deep-seated powers of being and of leading the individual beyond mere rationality.

Reality is made into symbols and symbols are made into reality. While symbols are not identical to that which they represent, they help to gain access to spiritual reality. The origin of symbols is extra-human: it lies in the establishment of a ritual act that can possess multiple meanings, meanings which are complementary rather than mutually contradictory, each being true and real according to the perspective adopted.

With the degeneration of symbolism, symbols become mere artistic or philosophical expressions incapable of awakening human consciousness through the power of imagery.

Myths, rites and symbols are all interconnected. Rites necessarily imply symbolism, while every symbol is a rite in itself, as it possesses an extra-human origin. Myth, frequently a dramatic tale of human life and its connection to underlying forces, serves as the 'logical' framework for the articulation of both rites and symbols.

APPENDIX I
THE SYMBOLISM OF THE CROSS

To understand the symbols of Tradition is to awaken primordial energy in oneself and to favour the renovation of one's being by re-establishing the order and authority that comes from the spirit.

The Cross is one of the most significant symbols, as it conceals the value of the Primordial Tradition. For this reason, the Cross is known as the universal symbol.

The Cross stands for the universal man: he who has defeated death and transcended the merely human existence based on instinct, thus having attained ultimate self-realisation. The Cross also stands for the Tree of Life, which lies at the centre of the world; hence, it alludes to the notion of centre and primordial purity. Two directions are expressed by the Cross: the horizontal and the vertical, both of which possess several meanings.

The Cross reconciles the opposition between the plane of manifestation (the horizontal axis) and the drive towards transcendence (the vertical axis). The Cross thus symbolises the unity in which different, distinct yet non-conflicting realties participate in an organic and complementary whole.

In anthropological terms,[21] the vertical axis stands for human personality, the self or soul: the active and eternal component of each creature. The vertical

---

[21]   The term 'anthropology' (from the Greek *anthropos* = 'man' + *logia*, which derives from *logein* = 'to say') is used to describe the study of the essential traits that characterise the life and behaviour of man. In the present context, the term alludes to the analogy between man and symbol: to the possibility of reading the symbolism of the Cross as an expression of human life.

direction is the domain of the sacred, which leads to the heavens but can also lead to the abyss. The horizontal axis, by contrast, stands for individuality, the ego, body and spirit: the passive and mortal component of each creature. This is the domain of historical becoming, in which ideologies and human elements clash. The two axes divide space and time into four equal parts, each of which represents an inner and outer reflection and can be read as a stage in human life. Each quarter thus stands for a crucial moment in human existence, time and space. Nature itself divides time and space into quarters: four are the cardinal points (north, east, south and west); four the elements of matter (fire, air, earth and water); and four are the divisions of terrestrial nature (mineral, plant, animal and human). Four too are the portions of the day (midnight, dawn, midday, sunset) and the seasons of each year. Similar fourfold partitions can be observed in other areas. The human body, for instance, can be divided into four chief parts: the head (brain, white), breast (heart, red), stomach (liver, black) and limbs (feet and hands). In accordance with this partition, the Indo-European peoples structured their social organisation into four castes (priests, warriors, producers, servants), above which stood the King.

Human life too is divided into four principal stages: the prenatal stage, birth, maturity and death.

APPENDIX II
THE SYMBOLISM OF THE SUN

The Sun is the heavenly body *par excellence:* its light and heat nourish the natural cycle and make life itself possible.

Ever since remote Antiquity, the Sun has been seen to symbolise the boundary between two realities: the luminous reality of life and spirituality on the one hand; and on the other, the dark nature of night and death.

The *Rig-veda*[22] states: 'In the visible Sun we adore the (invisible) Sun that has lit the Sun and all the other stars of the Sky.' Similarly, the seasons of the year or the hours of the day possess both external and internal manifestations, veritable 'analogies' of the stages of human life.

Many myths describe the process whereby man breaks free from his animal nature as a voyage that the soul makes from the Earth to the Sun through various planets and stars. The daily or yearly course of the Sun can be divided into four essential stages in which its light takes on different forms and meanings.

The first stage is dawn: the place and time of the visible birth of the Sun. The dawn shows the Sun rising from the horizon: that which was previously hidden is now made visible again. The Sun is born in the east and at the moment of the year that corresponds to the Spring Equinox. On this day light and darkness stand in equilibrium, for they are of the same duration; henceforth, darkness will diminish, yielding to the light of the Sun. At this time Nature awakens, all things

---

[22]   The *Rig-veda* is the first and oldest of the four *Vedas,* which together are the foundational texts of Hinduism. (Ed.)

renew themselves and bloom: that which is concealed manifests itself, and new life is born. For man, this is the best time for action.

The second stage is midday, when the light of the Sun has reached the apex of its radiance and energy. The Sun here stands at its zenith,[23] the highest point it can reach in its course. This stage corresponds to the south geographically, and to the Summer Solstice. This is the longest day of the year, when the Sun comes to symbolise the triumph of light over darkness, and the splendour and power of the soul. It is in this period of fertility and abundance that the fruits of what was previously sown are reaped, as exteriority and interiority – being and nature – stand in perfect unity and harmony.

According to cyclical doctrine, that which has reached its apex can only decline; hence, Nature at this stage gradually withers, as the days grow shorter and decline sets in.

The time and place of the retreat of the Sun is marked by sunset. Like at dawn, the Sun finds itself on the horizon; yet this time, its course proceeds in an opposite direction possessing an opposite symbolism, as life withdraws into itself. The Sun sets in the west and at the moment of the year that corresponds to the Autumn Equinox. As in spring, the day of the Equinox embodies the balancing of light and darkness; this time, however, it is night that will increase. As days grow shorter and Nature enters a phase of hibernation, light and life can be seen to withdraw. What was visible now conceals itself once more: the dark and cold season approaches. It is not by chance that the feasts held in this period are either those in remembrance of the dead or those connected to symbols of virility, purity

---

[23] Zenith: the point at which the vertical line traced by the observer meets the celestial sphere.

and light (St. Michael, St. Martin, the Immaculate Conception, St. Lucy).[24] The light of being vanishes from the outside, as if a slow death were enveloping the whole of Nature.

The fourth and final stage is midnight, when the Sun is no longer visible and coldness and darkness prevail. With its ice and snow this period is connected to the north geographically, and to the Winter Solstice. This is the longest night of the year, when the Sun reaches the lowest point on the horizon and darkness seems to have vanquished light. Yet, what has reached rock bottom can only rise upward and grow: a new ascendant phase thus begins. Days then grow longer and light overcomes darkness. Gradually, Nature awakens and the weather turns mild once more.

The Winter Solstice is a critical moment and a particularly dramatic symbol. It embodies the beginning of a new solar year and a new life (cycle), as an everlasting sign of rebirth and victory, and as a symbol of the strength of life that overcomes death.

As the Sun rises victorious over the darkness, so must man triumph against his mortal and instinctual nature.

---

[24]   St. Michael is identical with the Archangel Michael and is often considered the patron saint of warriors. St. Martin was a Roman soldier who converted to Christianity in the Fourth century and later became famous as a monastic bishop in present-day France. St. Lucy was another Fourth century Roman convert to Christianity who was martyred for her beliefs. (Ed.)

PART TWO:

THE FRONT
OF
TRADITION

1

IGNIS FATUUS[1]

We have long been silent witnesses to the painful inception – and frequent failure – of ventures of varying degrees of worth at the hands of groups of the so-called Radical Right. Like will-o'-the-wisps, these ventures are set alight only to be put out, draining enthusiasm, sapping energies and wasting human resources. Most people would lay the blame for this on the lack of suitable means and on the public's lack of interest in the issues addressed and solutions suggested by the Radical Right. What is certain is that this enduring scenario only helps our enemies, and threatens to lead us towards an irreversible rigor mortis.

In the light of the above considerations, it is clear that in order to remedy the situation it is necessary to shift our attention from the milieu and the methods adopted by it to the individuals themselves. Before outlining any kind of programme, it is necessary to select men worthy of their roles. This is only possible through an engagement with everyday reality capable of assessing the actual abilities, attitudes and *solar qualities* of each individual. The man who differentiates himself from the masses is he who is capable of acting in the modern world in an assertive and concrete way. Only a group formed by the willing association of men of this 'race' – men who have put themselves to the test by dominating rather than rejecting the outside world – will be capable of knowing how to act, with what means and strategy, and with the certainty of being something other than a mere will-o'-the-wisp.

---

[1]   Latin: 'will-o'-the-wisp', a name given to apparitions that sometimes appear over swampland. (Ed.)

2

EACH IN HIS PLACE

One of the defining traits of contemporary man is to see himself as something very important –indeed, indispensable; hence, the prevailing concern in all activities today is personal gain. This can easily be observed in everyday life (family, school, work, etc.). Modern man finds it impossible to engage in any task unless it is for material gain. Such a desire to nourish and aggrandise one's ego is the most evident sign of the inner squalor of modernity.

Regrettably, the same attitude is frequently found in the ranks of the Right. Many groups are formed under the leadership of small chiefs who feed their ego by sucking the lifeblood of their followers. The more imposing the attitude of these chiefs, the more passive that of the milieu in which they operate. When someone in such a group is seen to threaten the established 'leadership', the chief wages an internal war that inevitably leads to the fragmentation of the group itself.[2]

In order to genuinely act, it is necessary to radically change these attitudes, which do not befit the man of Tradition. One must rediscover the taste for impersonal action: action pursued not to fulfil psychological needs born of inner weaknesses, but regardless of any personal whims and expected results. For any action that is not stripped of personal, egoistic motives, is mere agitation,

---

[2] We have used the expression 'sucking the lifeblood' in this context, because the chiefs in question, like vampires drinking the blood of their victims, exploit the creativity, good faith and inner purity of their militants to aggrandise their own selves. The aptness of this metaphor will be appreciated as soon as one considers the history of the various movements of the Right, full of worthless men turned into legends.

which turns the individual into a passive recipient and victim of the action itself.

Our political milieu must allow any individual to 'rise' and take his rightful place, be it at the summit or lower rung of the hierarchical ladder. 'To each his own' must be the ruling principle that allows every militant to fully express his potential in the sphere that most suits him.

3

INTERIORISING THE DOCTRINE

Those seeking to serve Tradition and who are led by a higher drive to overcome the conditionings of everyday life must foster not merely their own intellectual formation – initially one seeks in books the answers he cannot find elsewhere – but also a progressive inner transformation. It is evident how individuals are often led to act by passions or mental processes that lack profound roots, and hence give rise to fleeting enthusiasms, soon destined to melt like snow. All this goes to prove the instability of contemporary vocations. What needs to be rediscovered is the genuine meaning of the word Culture as a form of action at the very core of one's own being. Culture means 'nurture': an inner growth and development that frees man from the slavery forced upon him. One must interiorise what notions he has progressively acquired, as to avoid turning traditional doctrine into something he has just read. It is necessary to grasp – almost instinctively – the demonic character of the modern world, without having to align oneself with the world of Tradition through mental, ideological reasoning. In this respect, anything can become a source of doctrine: doctrine can be acquired through first-hand experience. Every event can be seen as a symbol to be deciphered, and which can contribute to one's inner formation. By successfully interiorising doctrine, it is possible to avoid falling prey to foolish forms of external rigidity of an either purely formal or – what is worse – moralistic character, which have nothing to do with the human type of the differentiated man. By contrast, it will be necessary to render the core of our own being – the seat of the holy fire – as impenetrable as solid rock, if we are to resist the attacks waged by the modern world.

4

BEYOND IDEOLOGY

Ideology is a product of the modern world, and one of its most dangerous weapons.

Ideology is a wall erected by power, a crystal palace where man ceases to be active, aware and alive. Everything here has been thought out for him, organised, discussed and implemented. Responsibilities and creative actions have been delegated, so that man grows increasingly weak and useless: nothing but a vegetable. When one's mind escapes the control of ideology it is soon led back to the 'order' of quietness and mediocrity. Through ideology man is turned into a bourgeois, a mere unit, a proletarian.

Ideology, be it that of the ruling class or the opposition, makes man pliant by blocking his spontaneity, nature and dignity, turning him into a dull creature ready to drown in the grey squalor of sloth.

Through ideology, each man is assigned a place in the *danse macabre* of power.

The great sickles of ideological reapers always gather what philosophers and intellectuals have sown. While liberalism has absorbed the bourgeoisie, Marxism has described the most evident victims of capitalist progress: proletarians. Both liberalism and Marxism have served as the instruments of power. All wretched and subject peoples, who lack roots, traditions or hopes, meet their death through ideology, which divides, levels and rapes.

Revolution lies beyond all this. Revolution is not found in books, nor is it taught in schools: it grows and can be experienced every day by each militant. Revolution is reflected in one's land, in its songs and heroes. Revolution requires no codification, for it is implemented through man's nature as an untiring creator. Revolution does not give rise to new ideas: its idea is the fulfilment of the spiritual and material needs of the individual. Revolution knows neither classes nor class awareness, but only men: men who struggle to affirm their right to live according to nature, with their own folk, in their own land. Such is the organic view of life. The wall has failed to enclose us; now, it should expect no peace.

5

LIFESTYLE

Growing aware of traditional rules does not mean passively accepting them or superficially impressing them on one's mind so that they may then be reeled off in an attempt to seem wise. Rather, these rules must be assimilated and applied at every moment in one's life.

The Tradition we seek to experience is so alive and eternal that only the *living dead* will fail to grasp its relevance. Style is not something that can be purchased or something that grows on trees: it is the fruit of suffering, discipline and love. Thought and action must be turned into a lifestyle: we must qualify ourselves through our style rather than our words.

Suffering is the physical and particularly inner pain that puts human nature to the test. One must accept suffering and experience it in all its aspects: in the family, which seeks to stop us when our spirit is urging us to make certain choices; in society, which judges us because of the people we associate with or the 'reprehensible' acts we commit; in the physical exertion of a fight; and in the painful awareness of our own meanness and cowardice. Unless interiorised and overcome, all these aspects of life will crush us.

Discipline is the will to reach one's goal through perseverance, meticulousness and order. In order to march alongside his comrades, the warrior must train each day and promptly answer the orders of his superior; he must follow the rhythm that allows him to attune himself to the duty he is called to fulfil.

Love is the force that must guide man towards all higher goals. All acts are to be performed not for egoistic reasons, but rather in an impersonal fashion. Only by following these precepts can the aforementioned lifestyle be attained. To strive for this aim is to attempt to re-establish the inner balance that has long gone missing in man, overwhelmed as he is by the illusions of the modern world.

6
FIRM FOUNDATIONS

The process of dissolution is well underway. Both on a national and global level, society is about to disintegrate: everything suggests that the putrefying structure of society is coming to an end. The constant swing between moments of seeming calm and others of profound tension is indicative of the agony of society. And were events suddenly to escalate, the Front of Tradition would not be prepared to face the situation.

For this reason, it is necessary to act as witnesses of Tradition in an impersonal and flexible fashion that may allow us to infiltrate society at various levels. In collaboration with one another, the Operative Units of the Front of Tradition could engage in a number of activities. The Front of Tradition will only be established if each Unit, in accordance with its individual inclinations and characteristics, will act with heroic dedication. We have long emphasised the need to establish a firm foundation through men and resources capable of driving and sustaining the movement in the future, without further ado. What we mean by this is that we should avoid committing the same mistakes we have made in the past, which are all too evident to those who are not blinded by overzealousness and the thirst for power. There is much to learn from the past, even if new mistakes will probably be made in the future.

The suggestions made so far are aimed at defining the unified and original matrix that provides the foundation for the establishment of the movement. Without a sense of unity, nothing can be created – only countless and pointless suggestions formulated. The formation of Units will remain a utopian project as long as the true obstacles have not been removed. Only when there is a sense of genuine unity can endeavours and projects be directed towards a common goal; otherwise, each individual will pursue his own self-interest through social climbing – something that has nothing to do with comradeship. All this goes to show how muddled the Radical Right is when it comes to matters of strategy: means are here mistaken for ends and vice versa. Unless this obstacle is overcome, unless real unity is achieved, we will be wasting our time.

7

THE NEW MAN

EXISTENTIAL GUIDELINES
FOR MEMBERS OF AN OPERATIVE UNIT

Legionary life is beautiful. Yet it is not beautiful because of wealth, entertainments or luxury. It is beautiful because of the large number of dangers it poses; beautiful because of the noble comradeship that ties Legionaries of the whole country in a holy brotherhood of struggle; beautiful because of inflexible and virile bearing in the face of suffering. When a man joins the Legionary organisation, he must be aware of the life that awaits him, of the path he must follow...

The above passage is quoted from the writings of C.Z. Codreanu. It offers a complete picture of the kind of New Man the Legionary Movement aspired to create, and which our own vanguard aspires to today.

It is clear that a person who joins an Operative Unit must already be aware of the kind of life that awaits him. It is also true, however, that until this life is experienced through action, it will only be known on a vague conceptual level. To get a sense of what this life is like, it is necessary to develop a certain maturity: to lay some basic foundations, so to speak.

Codreanu describes three tests the Legionary must pass, and which correspond to three inner conditions that must be attained. These three conditions are metaphorically described as the 'mountain of suffering', the 'forest of wild beasts' and the 'swamp of dejection'.

First test: the 'mountain of suffering'. This test takes its name from its aim, which is to sever the personal ties that bind us as individuals and limit our potential for action: family ties, for instance, or those of passion and bourgeois contamination. To embark on this test is to climb a mountain that grows increasingly steep. Only those endowed with a strong spirit of sacrifice will be capable of reaching the summit. Rather than being based on any external action, this first test is derived from an inner action that seeks to provide a new existential foundation through the values of love, honour and loyalty.

Second test: once the values of love, honour and loyalty have been assimilated, it is necessary to face external reality: everyday life (here described as the 'forest of wild beasts') in the modern world, which constantly attempts to instil conformity in those who do not feel at home within it. Facing and overcoming danger is part of the Legionary lifestyle, which leaves little room for cowardice. This is a way of putting to the practical test what has initially been absorbed only intellectually.

Third test: the 'swamp of dejection' symbolises the inner condition of those who have embarked on the journey only to stop, either because they are unable to see what lies ahead of them, or because they believe that the struggle will not yield any positive result. The image of the swamp perfectly encapsulates the inner condition of a man stuck in a muddy terrain hostile to any rapid and incisive action, where the essential value of loyalty is lost.

While these three tests are listed separately, they actually represent conditions that manifest themselves simultaneously. The inner formation of the militant must be measured through an engagement with external reality right from the start, if it is to transcend the merely conceptual level; as for dejection, it can manifest itself in relation to both internal or external action. By passing these three tests, the militant embraces a lifestyle that allows him, in the words of Julius Evola, to 'newly awaken from within, take a form, and establish an inner sense of order and rectitude within oneself'.

8

A FIGHTING VANGUARD

The present historical phase would seem to leave little leeway for any attempt to awaken the new generations from their slumber. It is clear that we are living in times of transition and that this period of stagnation will not last forever. There is a discernible uneasiness in the air, born of the sense of futility that characterises contemporary life. As the wheel of history continues to spin, a new time of dissent will come to shake what at present appears to be a social order so firmly entrenched as to leave little scope for possible change. Yet, against all appearances, uneasiness does exist in our society: anger in response to the way in which imposed models have come to condition our life is destined to explode.

Given the current situation, it is worth considering what the function of the Traditional Vanguard might be. The duty of this Vanguard is to be prepared for the moment when rage will erupt in society, when what will be needed, aside from plans, will be men capable of channelling dissent, not by manipulating it, but by directing it towards the only values capable of justifying revolt: the search for inner freedom. Today's action must aim at tomorrow's victory: the victory that the Traditional Vanguard must strive towards every day. At present, the role of the Vanguard is to pave the way for this great event.

The duty of the Vanguard is to foster development within its ranks by finding new militants and putting them to the test; by making not blind followers of orders of these men but warriors conscious of the role that will be theirs: that of future leaders.

It is essential that each individual be allowed to act in accordance with his vocation.

A firm economic foundation must also be provided through internal taxation – in the form of a sizable personal contribution – and militant intervention in the organisation of those activities that allow political affairs to proceed unimpeded. Means of propaganda must be refined and tested over and over again, until made perfect.

Such must be the role of the genuine Traditional Vanguard. It requires men to make a choice between what truly matters and what is merely superfluous or instrumental; men who must possess an iron will, as well as a fanatical faith in the fact that victory is possible and nothing can stop the affirmation of our vertical ideal of life.

9

THE RECTIFICATION
OF THE INDIVIDUAL

There are moments of lucidity in life when a person realises how futile the pursuit of the false aims and achievements of everyday routine actually are. In these cases, the most common reaction is a sense of nausea and distressing bewilderment, followed by a desire to change one's life. Yet, if the person in question fails to find a solution to the sense of squalor that afflicts his life beyond the ordinary channels that allow individuals to vent their frustration, he will soon fall back into his sad and monotonous pattern of existence.

While this is what occurs in most cases, there are some exceptions. Some individuals do not acquiesce to the idea of living what they perceive as an alien life, and with great toil succeed in turning their destructive impulse into a constructive one.

Clearly, given that we are dealing here with feelings and personal reactions, each case will be different: in order to clarify matters, it is necessary to present what is only a schematic picture. Some individuals, driven by enthusiasm, will desperately struggle to achieve their plans; yet when faced with various obstacles in the realisation of their small, everyday goals (not to mention in their attempt to bestow a higher meaning on life!), will ultimately give up and either get back in line or lose their minds. Others, by contrast, manage to keep their wits about them and prove capable of coolly assessing the prospect of realising their dreams, thus laying the foundations for a concrete project.

10
ACTION

In what follows an attempt is made to render less abstract the human relationship between the various members of the Operative Unit, which is to say relationships within the community that, with wilfulness and dedication, embraces this project. Moreover, an attempt will be made to provide a simple outline of the essential traits each community and member operating along the Front of Tradition must possess. The primary aim here is to overcome the corpse-like immobility that characterises the Radical Right by helping define the organisational and particularly existential guidelines on which the action of each group depends. To integrate these brief notes, we suggest reading *The Nest Leader's Manual* by Corneliu Zelea Codreanu, Captain of the Rumanian Iron Guard.[3]

EXISTENTIAL GUIDELINES

It is easy to see how society is becoming increasingly characterised by an individual lack of discipline and drive towards the holy. Often without realising it, we are affected by negative influences that stain our actions with the kind of fickleness, hypocrisy and dishonesty we readily identify as the traits of the kind of personality we wish to fight.

---

[3]   Corneliu Codreanu, *The Nest Leader's Manual* (CZC Books, 2005). (Ed.)

The need thus arises for an inner action capable of removing the deadweight that stifles our personal growth and halts our upward drive. To pursue this action is to foster a specific character and style within oneself day by day: to shape one's life, that is, through the assimilation of Traditional values.

Each member of the Operative Unit must thus seek to rectify his own behaviour in such a way as to do away with all signs of vulgarity and unseemliness; at the same time, he must develop a genuine aversion to all lies and betrayal. The militant will avoid the traps laid by the System in order to stunt possible changes: he will thus reject drugs and perversions. The militant will not abuse alcohol or engage in foolish and random acts of violence, which are but signs of human meanness and cowardice. Similar deviances are the most evident manifestations of a world in ruins and of a type of human being that gives up on life, as he is incapable of self-control.

The starting point for any attempt to 'conquer' oneself is the leading of a 'normal and orderly' life: the conquering of everyday reality by assigning life its true meaning. What matters is not what one does, but how one does it. Thus relations with one's family, girlfriend or friends, as well as work and study commitments – not to mention one's active engagement as a militant – will have to be experienced in a new light, where individual responsibility and sacrifice take the place of all arbitrariness and emotionality. In his interactions in the above social fields, the individual must undergo a radical change: sentimentality and bourgeois conformity must be replaced by loyalty, clarity and sincerity. The obstacles and difficulties encountered in everyday life should thus be envisaged as a useful occasion to put oneself to the test. Only on the basis of reactions and behaviours can a person assess his own limits and abilities.

The above kind of work allows the individual to discover his own nature. Through similar tests and through self-observation each person can measure the extent to which he is under the spell of the modern world. Lazy personalities will be forced to react with greater perseverance, while the more frantic ones will have to limit their own enthusiasm. Rising early in the morning, for instance, and not going to bed late will contribute to regulate the militant's personal conduct by disciplining his life in accordance with the daily rhythms of the cosmic order. What we are dealing with here is a gradual inner reconstruction, to be implemented through small progressive steps: small and apparently insignificant actions which, once interiorised, can lead to great achievements.

While living in a so-called state that is completely deprived of superior points of references, the member of an Operative Unit will find the necessary support to resist and strengthen himself within his own community. For such a man life becomes a 'soldier's service' marked by incessant struggle. On the one hand are Tradition, justice and Truth, on the other anti-Tradition, abuse and falsehood: two opposite fronts. Unless a person leads a righteous life, he will easily fall prey to the enemy's seductions. For it is often the case that an individual, while acting with good intentions, becomes an instrument of subversion, as he fails to interiorise certain values and strengthen his self-identity.

When dealing with oneself a firm line must be adopted: the decadence of the world and its lost souls must be faced with the greatest resoluteness. The line drawn between ourselves and our enemies must distance us from all external influences and from our own petty egoism. Only in such a way will the individual conquer his own self and forge a character capable of fostering genuine spiritual renewal. The individual thus becomes a model for others: a real man capable of acting as a witness and of sharing his own personal experience.

ORGANISATIONAL GUIDELINES

'Operative Unit' is the term we use to describe a body of men who operate within society by taking part in a unitary and organic political project. To resist all superficiality, the Operative Unit must take the values of Tradition as its models; it must aim to educate individuals and find men of a similar character through its active presence in society, by acting as a witness and an example. Truth, loyalty, honour, justice and sacrifice will be the core principles in the formation of each militant.

Right from the start, every member must be conscious of the need to do away with the allurements of the modern world; the choice to join an Operative Unit calls for total commitment, a commitment which also affects so-called private life.

No one must be forced to stick to his choice: militancy is a free decision; the dedication of each individual will serve as a test for his feelings and maturity. It will then be a matter of honour whether one pursues his tasks and duties with the greatest care and energy, even when he does not feel like it or is facing what appear to be insurmountable obstacles. Nothing can be achieved without sacrifice: the path of Tradition calls for selfless action. By contrast, those who will continue acting selfishly will soon feel the need to abandon their Unit. Sacrifice will be integrated by an essential tool of solidarity within the Unit: personal discussion among militants. This discussion will not take the form of a confession or psychoanalytical session; rather, it will seek to overcome the bourgeois inclination to regard one's private life as inviolable. It is difficult to be a good judge of oneself when living alone; a community instead provides the opportunity for a fair discussion based on the exchange of personal experiences and aimed at furnishing advice which allows all comrades to get to know each other and personally improve. It will thus be necessary to point to the errors of those who are following the same path as us, were they to behave in manners not befitting a man of Tradition. We should not worry about hurting the feelings of our comrades by pointing out their failings, for what might seem as a poison at first will soon act as a medicine for those conscious of their own mistakes. In learning how to interiorise the advice he receives, a person is strengthened and afforded the chance to triumph over the problems brought to light. Those who on the contrary dislike this method will be asked to leave, as they evidently ignore the meaning of the term 'comradeship'. Most people are unable to see the free exchange of opinions among comrades as a necessary act of love for the formation of the individual; rather, they perceive it as an intrusion in one's private sphere. Yet it is only through this act of love that unconquerable unity will be established in a Unit, by doing away will all egoistic drives towards gossip and inner polemic. Mutual help and warning comrades about their failings are ways of experiencing community to the fullest extent. Particular attention must be paid to avoid any sloppy sentimentality: for dedication towards one's comrade must be based on an awareness of treading the same path as him, motivated by the same ideals and desire to implement them.

Having outlined some basic practices, we can now turn to the inner structure and activities of each Operative Unit. Operative Units are marked by regular duties and deadlines that should not be abandoned or neglected if not in emergencies. A ritual significance must be assigned to the meeting of the community at a fixed time and day, to the giving of a financial contribution amounting to 10% of one's monthly earnings, to the acceptance of responsibilities as a way of measuring one's readiness for self-sacrifice and action in the name of oneself, the group and the Ideal. Missed appointments, lack of punctuality, attachment to money and 'personal' things cannot be tolerated. One must be strict with those intolerant of these rules, which infuse action with order and cleanse the individual.

In the course of every meeting, the tasks assigned to each militant, the results achieved and the difficulties encountered will all be reviewed. Suggestions for the improvement of the group will also be brought forward. Current events will be discussed in order to provide militants with points of reference. The reading of traditional works, and particularly the writings of R. Guénon and J. Evola, will prove useful in this respect. Attention must be paid, however, not to fall prey to an arid intellectualism incapable of translating the written word on the level of action.

In the achievement of the goals mentioned so far, a central role will be played by the 'head' of the group, who must act as a constant presence and driving force for all militants. Through his way of life, the Leader must show militants the path they must follow. He who serves as the 'regent' of an Operative Unit must possess the virtues of the New Man, thus acting as an exemplar for the rest. Among the chief duties of the Leader is to guard the group against all perils, and particularly all forms of degeneration, such as the perversion of the sense of hierarchy. This occurs when individual roles within the group come to be seen as goals in themselves, and when they do not match actual individual qualifications. Groups where this perverse attitude spreads turn into military barracks ruled by tyranny and paternalism, where those truly able are denied the chance to affirm themselves. Hierarchy, it will be worth recalling, is not a bureaucratic ladder that can be ascended according to one's years of service; hierarchy, first and foremost, means quality: the Leader is he who most clearly embodies the values of Tradition and acts as an exemplar for others.

We should now spend a few words on the external activities an Operative Unit will have to engage in, in order to affirm itself beyond a small circle of personal acquaintances. The duty of each Unit is to define a plan and assess the means to pursue chosen goals. The economic sphere is certainly among the first issues a group must address, as in a world where everything revolves around money even the simplest of political battles entails a degree of financial expenditure. This does not mean that the purpose of economic activities must be financial gain; rather, financial gain must be a means to secure effective political engagement. This sort of activity makes it possible to measure individual commitment and the progressive development of the group in a very concrete way.

Even when a powerful structure has been established, it is necessary to always bear in mind the reasons that led to its foundation in the first place: the affirmation of the values of Tradition and the formation of individual militants. Our aim is not to become good entrepreneurs, but to achieve complete independence in this world.

There are many activities that need to be organised: while each person can operate more efficiently in his own local area, it is essential to establish a network to spread the culture of Tradition. The primary duty of each Operative Unit would have to be to open bookshops or centres of book distribution in every city that still lacks such resources. Where this is not possible, it will be necessary to hand out textual material to existing bookshops or places (such as libraries) that can distribute it.

These are only some of the organisational suggestions that have been successfully adopted in the past and which continue to bear fruits today. We are conscious of the fact that such a project cannot be the monopoly of any one person or group, for it ought to be shared by all those who seek to nourish their inner fire through sacrifice and love by working to establish the Front of Tradition.

THE MEANING OF BROTHERHOOD

What do we mean by the word 'brotherhood'? Is this a spontaneous relation among different individuals or is it something we must strive to develop? The answer is that it is both: it is a spontaneous relation among blood relations, but it is also an attempt to embrace a new life through a common sensibility. From our perspective, brotherhood is what links those individuals who cherish the same pure ideals of faith, justice, fortitude, temperance and – more generally – virtue. No doubt, individuals can be brothers in betrayal, injustice, weakness and intemperance: in this case they would also be united, but under the banner of vice rather than superior ideals. Yet any form of brotherhood is deficient unless it is based on certain ideals. It is these ideals that give meaning to brotherhood: if the latter offers a form and body, the former represent the substance and spirit.

In a positive sense, therefore, we see brotherhood as something that must be established, for we are not linked to one another by ties of blood. Ours are ties that must be developed through sacrifice and struggle, and through the ideals that unite us.

If by 'brotherhood' we merely refer to collective good humour, to shared food and conversation, to something devoid of any concrete, operative reference to ideals, then there will be no means of advancing further: at best, we will remain in the same situation; at worst, we will lose all sense of unity. For it is possible for individuals to become brothers in a negative sense, if they unite out of fear of being alone, in order to have some allies when they need them, or – what is even worse – to exploit one another for selfish ends. In these and similar cases the brotherhood established is not a sincere one: individuals end up justifying misdeeds both great and small, and the group becomes an excuse for petty behaviour. Another risk is to seek understanding only amongst members of the group, which soon leads to sectarianism: alongside the individual ego a collective one will thus be formed, which is even harder to get rid of. In cases such as this it is preferable to remain alone, or at least to establish a new group that might take a positive direction, embarking on a difficult journey.

The path of knowledge is by nature a solitary one. If one seeks to pursue it with others whom he wishes to make his brothers, he must adhere to ideals and values that the ego is quite reluctant to accept. For members of a group to become brothers of the spirit, each must focus on his own inner development; forms of passionate – not to mention morbid – attachment to others are wrong, insofar as they establish new bonds, whereas the path of freedom should lead to the disintegration of all bonds of attachment. We must thus realise that spiritual brotherhood will only ever come into being when someone in the group can claim to embody its ideals. Until that happens, the only claim that can legitimately be made is that of being acquaintances or friends who seek to *become* brothers of the spirit.

One must be particularly wary of presumptuousness, which is among the most common faults in modern man (and we ourselves should assume to be modern men, until proven wrong). It is not spiritual brotherhood that should be taken for granted, but rather the lack thereof, if we are to avoid developing another collective ego – the ideal ground for the subversion of ideals. Brotherhood is something that must be achieved through constant sacrifices and the unifying values of faith, justice, fortitude and temperance (just again to emphasise the virtues we previously mentioned). Devoid of ideals, brotherhood can only subsist in a negative sense. So we should now turn to consider these ideals in more detail.

Faith and justice are expressed through hierarchy, which sets aims that are different from those of the ego – one's most bitter enemy – and delivers a hard blow to any sense of self-importance. Fortitude is developed through hard work, which similarly delivers a hard blow to passiveness and laziness. Temperance is achieved by avoiding impulsive reactions dictated by passion, and carrying out one's duties. It is worth recalling here that it is easier to justify all vices when alone: those who wish to live in a traditional community ought to avoid this kind of self-justification and face their own weaknesses. It is thus necessary to be in the company of men who are far from compliant, and who might come across as unpleasant because of their frankness. The potentially misleading notion of kindness should here be replaced by justice. As members of a group, it is our duty to trust the Leader and always keep the fundamental values in mind. Only in such a way will we become brothers of the spirit capable of achieving freedom and victory.

11

THE COMMUNITY

Modern sociology – following Ferdinand Tönnies[4] – distinguishes between the notions of community and society. The term 'community' applies to a natural, spontaneous and organic grouping of people, based on ties of blood. The community is a living organism with a given heritage from which members derive a sense of solidarity and belonging: the feeling of belonging to an organic reality. Society, by contrast, is a rationally organised grouping established for the achievement of concrete goals. Society is not based on any shared cultural or natural heritage, but rather on shared aims. As such, it is an artificial construct devoid of natural ties, a distinctive tradition and organic unity. Society springs from an illusory 'social contract' (such

---

[4]   Ferdinand Tönnies (1855-1936) is often regarded as the first German sociologist. He is best remembered for the distinction he drew between community, which he defined as the types of relationships that existed within families and villages in traditional settings, and society, which he saw exemplified in the modern state or corporations. He believed that this distinction came about as a result of a different understanding of one's place; in communities, individuals think of themselves in relation to the group, while in societies individuals only think of how to advance their own self-interest. (Ed.)

as the liberal principle of mutual exchange – *do ut des*[5] rather than from bonds of solidarity. Human relations in society are thus regulated by 'market laws' (free enterprise, utilitarianism, profit), and marked by anonymity and individualism. The notion of society, as such, not only lacks any superior point of reference, but sees morality itself as subservient to economic principles.

We have touched upon the distinction between community and society in order to move beyond merely theoretical discussions. Yet, we should also point out that both kinds of human groupings are ultimately foreign to the traditional, normal model of social organisation. The traditional model is neither a naturalist one (community: family, race, folk) nor a rationalist one (society: enterprise); rather, it is a qualitative, hierarchical model, based on laws ordained from above. In this case, one may speak of a 'society of men', 'elite' or 'Order'.

Given the above premise, which should help dispel any ambiguity, what we mean by 'traditional community' is any aristocratic and heroic organisation, the most strikingly embodiment of which is the ideal of Imperium (power from above).

*　　*　　*　　*　　*

The community plays a crucial role, insofar as it allows the individual to actually experience what would otherwise remain an intellectual abstraction. By use of the term 'community' we are thus referring not to a closed group of individuals incapable of affirming

---

5　　Latin: 'I give so that you may give.' (Ed.)

itself in the outside world, but rather to a group of men capable of offering an alternative to contemporary society and its bourgeois morality: a genuine social and political workshop. We believe that such a community would represent a means not to escape reality, but to affirm a truly revolutionary ideal: that of the fighting vanguard.

Regrettably, in the few groups where an attempt is being made today to unite individuals on the basis of ideals, communal spirit is not what it ought to be. The notion of community in this case becomes an excuse for evasion and the justification of one's limits, rather than an attempt to establish a differentiated human reality. For when speaking of community, it is necessary to bear in mind the kind of men who should comprise it: differentiated men. In everyday life, the individual is forced to come to terms with forms of behaviour that on a mental level he claims to reject and fight: vulgarity, misguided ambition, egoism, disloyalty, etc. One must admit that although we may claim the values of Tradition as our points of reference and models, we are all children of the modern world, and we live constantly surrounded by contradictions. The lack of an inner dimension, or the incapacity to accept Tradition as a law are the major causes of our inconsistency: we thus stand in need of corrective action. Action, however, is made even more difficult by the fact that the political and cultural milieu that should foster it has degenerated and is incapable of acting as an exemplar to follow.

The time has come, therefore, to make some radical choices, to either embrace or reject Tradition: there can be no middle ground. A man is only free insofar as he can choose; and each choice entails responsibility – in this case, a commitment to one's duties and respect for the sacred norms of Tradition. The only man who can truly be free is the man of Tradition, who accepts its norms and freely obeys them, thus attaining fulfilment. These are the necessary conditions to rediscover one's being beyond all conditioning, prejudices and habits. Inner reconstruction entails ridding oneself of conditioning superstructures. Unless this is achieved, our good intentions will bear no fruits. Once we have defined what we wish to do and who we aim to be, we will need to act accordingly. An individual does not excel because he goes to a particular pub or hangs out with the right crowd: excellence is achieved by living daily in accordance with what we purport to be.

THE TASKS OF THE COMMUNITY

The first task is to form men through impersonal action, by making them act without attachment to the fruits of action or any sense of gratification. It is all too often the case that we overlook our own whims and arbitrariness: we must instead put aside any desire to be in the limelight in favour of a clear-headed assessment of the events we are experiencing, shunning transient excitement and tearful attempts at self-justification. We must seek to limit all sources of distraction and superficiality, of disorder and lack of self-control, thus overcoming all strife, hypocrisy and falsehood. Individual adherence to a traditional community entails work of personal development aimed at achieving the desired condition of being through the necessary act of inner reconstruction.

Another task of the community is to bear witness. This consists in a guiding action aimed at perfectly embodying the values embraced. Ruling out any desire to proselytise, an attempt will be made to implement the principles of Tradition within the community itself, thus making it a centre of aggregation. Such a community will represent not the final goal, but rather a stage in one's personal development: the group will thus be comprised of members united by the same values and desire to implement a common project. It is important to understand that the community can be used as a tool and a shelter while ultimately embodying neither of these two things: rather, the community should be seen as an indispensable testing ground from which to strive for higher goals.

12

THE OPERATIVE UNIT

The establishment of democratic, popular and liberal systems, the embracing of coloured peoples, and the dulling of conscience among younger generations are but signs of one phase in the process of subversion. The end of this phase will reflect a change in the tactics and operative means adopted by the agents of subversion to deliver their final attack before the closing stage of the cycle.

The political Right is currently unprepared to face such an attack. Its young militants, even when acting in good faith, are continuously betrayed by the men who represent them and who are meant to guide their political action.

The present atomisation of the milieu that has Tradition as its reference point rules out the possibility of any close strategic planning, which necessarily implies a detailed definition of the revolutionary process.

In order to avoid the kind of misunderstanding that is often fostered by forms of intellectual traditionalism, it is necessary for each militant to become aware of his own aspirations and spiritual drive: to overcome all partiality by making his conduct impersonal and acknowledging the kind of communal forces capable of evaluating his attitudes and contributing to his inner development.

Only the presence of these factors can bestow legitimacy on any attempt at the hands of existing Units to affect chosen areas through cautious intervention: for individual attitudes and personal dispositions must be taken into account to make any action decisive. In the present society, which is marked by mass organisation and propaganda, one must be realistic about the limiting factors that condition the actions of militants, even when these individuals appear to possess the right personal attitudes and suitable means. All excessive enthusiasm and facile optimism must be done away with, and it is also necessary to protect oneself against the reactions that are likely to follow any such action.

Through a process of spontaneous action, the presence of Operative Units in a social and political context that appears irredeemably lost will become evident. It will be necessary, therefore, to establish a connection between existing Units: to define their various areas of intervention and take account of the different dispositions of the militants which comprise them in order for their actions to be rendered more effective.

Only when such Operative Units will be ready – and thus capable of directing all actions towards a single goal – will a detailed strategic plan be drafted. The various stages in the implementation of this plan will require careful analysis and a meticulous definition of the different phases in the fight for Tradition. If new

Operative Units are eventually added to the existing ones in order to establish a potent force, it will then be possible to start discussing their organic unity. This notion implies the existence of a spiritual centre which guides the actions of men who seek to shape existing reality with their presence, which in turn will foster the development of new Operative Units. Such are the necessary steps that must be taken towards the construction of a genuine elite.

The process leading to Organic Unity will be a slow yet inexorable one, provided we do not give up after the first difficulty we encounter, compromise with the falsehood of our enemies, or bask in the glory of any result achieved (which will always be but a small step forward in the long path that lies ahead of us).

Faced with a wall of lies and deceit, and also with vile attacks against the purity of our youth, the militant will be forced to come to terms with his own human condition and discover the sense of sacrifice that ennobles it.

13

BEFORE THE MOVEMENT

In the so-called milieu of the Right, the question is periodically posed concerning the establishment of a unified movement: a movement capable of taking into account the political experiences of the past, while transcending them in order to resolutely face the challenges of the future.

The fact that a need for such a movement is felt is a positive thing in itself: it is the sign of a process of maturation in our milieu which, in order to not be confined to partial and outdated political expressions, strives towards the Front of Tradition.

A unified movement, however, can only arise if it is capable of affirming itself in society as a historical manifestation of the doctrinal corpus of Tradition. This corpus must be actualised as far as possible through an action testifying to eternal, immutable and sacred principles which actually require no historical validation: for these will always retain their normative value, despite the unworthiness of the human actions inspired by them. The value of the movement, therefore, will depend on its capacity to adhere to and actualise the normative principles of Tradition. Only on the basis of this premise will it be possible to start planning the form and structure the movement might take.

It is worth stressing once more that both individual existence and the organisational forms that spring from it must be firmly anchored to Tradition. It is thus necessary to grasp the profound meaning of Evola's saying that: 'Before concerning oneself with external actions, which are often born of a temporary enthusiasm devoid of deep roots, one should work on himself by means of an action directed against all that is formless, elusive or bourgeois.'[6]

---

[6]   This quote comes from an interview with Evola that was published in *Ordine Nuovo* in January-February 1964, and later republished as part of an appendix to the Italian edition of *Ride the Tiger*. An English translation of the entire interview is available at the *Evola as He Is* Web site (http://thompkins_cariou.tripod.com/id20.html). (Ed.)

14
THE FUTURE IS NOW

SUGGESTIONS FOR AN ATTEMPT AT
POSSIBLE RECONSTRUCTION:
STRATEGIC CHOICES AND POLITICAL PRAXIS

CLARIFICATION

What follows derives from an assessment of reality based on personal, first-hand experience; as such, it is open to future changes and contributions. Its purpose is to provide a starting point inspired exclusively by the values of faith, loyalty and honour, in line with a worldview that assigns primacy of place to the sacred within a sphere of manifestation that also includes human existence.

PRELIMINARY REMARKS

In any evaluation of the objective possibilities of launching new forms of political action, a crucial role is played by a balanced assessment of the past. It is necessary to be aware of the fact that one's identity derives from the progressive flow of time and a series of experiences that are tied to personal inner conditions and, as such, are largely unrepeatable or, at any rate, of little value for any attempt at progress.

The living memory of the past, strengthened by a detailed analysis of past events and an ability to look towards the future, must lead us to avoid making any choices that experience (either direct or indirect) has already shown to be fruitless.

INDISPENSABLE CONDITIONS

The analysis of the recent past, the evaluation of experience and the study of history all lead to a series of observations that provide a peremptory affirmation of the indispensable conditions that must be met in order to attempt any restoration. The vileness of contemporary man can only lead to a repeat of what is already before our eyes. Hence, nothing will ever be possible unless the moral conscience of man is reaffirmed through the connection to a living centre. This is the primary aim each human community must strive for. Man has two options: transcendence or degradation.

THE INCIDENTAL

If one is aware of what must be preserved of the past and is conscious of the present situation, it will be easy for him to see that, in what we refer to as 'our milieu', people obstinately tend to make the same choices, which often appear quite illogical and completely out of touch with reality. Those who make such choices must be divested of their power and prevented from taking part in any attempt to construct a qualitative force capable of asserting itself in the future. To operate in such a way is to already be living in the future.

DAY ONE OF THE YEAR ZERO

THE AIM

The problem we face is to regain, or rather reassert, the world of Tradition.

This is our highest, most legitimate and concrete aspiration.

It is clear that the attainment of the highest goal necessarily entails the unfolding of countless underlying processes: if correctly planned and worked out, these will make the attainment of the final goal of restoration possible, *with the indispensable aid of the Divine Will*. It is important to emphasise here that once the final goal has been defined, and the most immediate aims have been set, one can only imagine what our present condition allows us to understand and imagine, if we are to stick to reality and avoid falling prey to idealistic delusions. The subsequent stages in the process of restoration will have to be defined as we move along, as the horizons of our imagination – which will develop an increasing ability to predict the future – will have broadened further.

REORGANISING RESIDUAL FORCES

It is first necessary to polarise the residual forces: all those who still seek a way of breaking free of the current bonds of human society, as well as those who could contribute towards a creative drive that would stir the more 'timid' people. The aim must be to bring about a creative change of direction – outside imposed

79

frameworks, confining labels or conditionings. At the present time, if we only cultivate our own backyard (our private life or social circle) and ignore any wider perspective, it will inevitably lead to our fall. Those who are acting as Leaders today should be aware of this fact, if they are to allow each militant within their own communities to 'grow' and form cadres capable of implementing the vigorous action required in the future.

RESIST TO EXIST

Once we have measured our strengths and weaknesses, as well as the abyss that must be crossed before we have the right to call ourselves revolutionaries, the need will increasingly arise for us to find new supporters. These must first be sought among the *garrisons* located on the border between oblivion and the hope of rebirth. It is necessary to gather all those active in this *frontier zone* around an operative plan in which differences of origin and identity will serve to define new means of constructive exchange and intervention: petty egoism must be overcome if we are to face our most sly and powerful enemy.

A primary need of ours, and one that cannot be delayed, is to erect efficient barriers of resistance to halt the corrosive action that is spreading in an all too systematic way, dividing and dispersing its potential opponents. Equally pressing is the need to strengthen our ranks through unwavering faith: faith in the fact that 'the force we wish to serve as instruments is eternally invincible'.[7]

---

[7]   From an article by Iron Guard leader Ion Mota, quoted by Corneliu Codreanu in *For My Legionaries,* p. 164. (Ed.)